Our Hollywood Tales

A MEMOIR

By

Bob & Anita Puglisi

S oc –
I hope you enjoy
our story.
Bob Puglisi
Anita Puglisi

Dedicated to our good friend and fellow writer Tara Untiedt. She was an actress, writer, director, and producer. Unfortunately, she left this world too soon, and her dreams went unfulfilled. She was always supportive and inspiring. She will be missed.

Also by Bob Puglisi

Novels
Railway Avenue
Midnight Auto Supply
Unassisted Living
The Hanalei House

Memoir
Almost A Wiseguy

INTRODUCTION

"I'd love to read your autobiography." That's what my friend, Lynda Jackson Petito, a DJ, writer, theatre director, and Italian American *paisan,* once said to me. Her statement surprised me, maybe naively, because I had never thought of my life as being very interesting, which I told her. Over the years, I have thought about what she said, so I decided to write about a time in my life that readers might enjoy. This story includes Anita, my wife of over forty-five years; it is impossible not to include her. With Anita's help, I have written most of the book, but she has pitched in writing the chapters about her career. The book talks about when we lived and worked in Hollywood, and I pursued acting and screenwriting, and Anita worked in TV and film production.

When I created my website, **www.bobpuglisi.com**, in the summer of 2019, I thought about including a blog. I was hesitant because I didn't think anyone would read it and didn't know if I could sustain writing a blog regularly. So I started reluctantly and put my blogs into four categories: Writing/Publishing; Random Thoughts; Hollywood Tales, and News. To my surprise, people have read them, and Hollywood Tales have been the most popular. When I mentioned that to Anita, she said, "People always like stories about Hollywood." I'm thankful to my blog readers and followers because you gave me the confidence to make this book possible.

Anita and I met in Manhattan in an Upper East Side singles bar called Little Johns. It was in the early 1970s. We had a brief encounter at the bar while buying drinks in the jam-packed establishment on a Friday night. She told me, "I'm here with my ex-boyfriend and some girlfriends."

Before our pleasant conversation ended, I asked her for her phone number. As the story goes, I met two other women at the same watering hole that night.

I wasn't interested in seeing either of them after a first date. Finally, I called Anita. She lived near Coney Island in Brooklyn, and I lived in Staten Island, a short drive over the Verrazano Bridge. She looked so lovely when she opened the door; she took my breath away. I had almost forgotten how pretty she was with her cute face framed by a head of beautiful shiny black hair. From behind Anita, a woman's voice said, "Bring him in! Let's see what he looks like!" I felt a little uncomfortable. I hadn't dated since I was in my late teens. At the time, I was in my mid-twenties. It took some getting used to, and it had been a long time since I had to meet a date's parents.

It was clear from that first meeting that her mom, Mary Cannarili, an energetic, short, plump little lady was the matriarch that ran the family. Cosmo, Anita's father, was quiet, reflective, wore black-rimmed, thick-lensed glasses, and had thinning hair. I survived the introduction, and we went out for the evening.

I took Anita to Staten Island to a nightclub I liked called Hadar. (I once tried to pick up Tito Puente's wife there while Tito and his band performed on stage. His beautiful lady sweetly informed me of my blunder.)

I wanted to be honest and felt compelled to tell Anita about my marital situation. "I'm separated from my wife, and we're getting a divorce." Anita's expression changed, but she didn't say anything. I continued, "I have a six-year-old daughter."

Anita looked at me reluctantly and said, "My sister, Mary, married a divorced guy. He has a kid too. My father disowned her and didn't want to see them."

I figured she was about to tell me she couldn't see me anymore, but she didn't.

She said, "My mother sneaks over to see them any chance she gets. She hopes my father will come around eventually."

I liked Anita very much and wanted to see more of her, but I worried that my marital problems would jeopardize our relationship.

Nevertheless, Anita and I continued dating, and we grew closer. A few weeks later, we went out for New Year's Eve. That's when I met her sister and brother-in-law, Joe Cannella. We went to an American Legion in Long Island, where their band, The Top Hats, was the night's entertainment. Years earlier, Anita and her sister had a rock and roll band called The Satin Dolls. Anita was the drummer; Mary, the band leader, played the organ; and their friend, Marilyn, played guitar and sang vocals. In the Top Hats, Joe Cannella was the saxophone player and singer, Mary was on her Hammond B3 organ, and they also had a guitar player and drummer.

When Anita and I started dating, I was a Computer Systems Programmer working for the New York Federal Reserve Bank. Anita worked at CBS as a secretary to the head of Radio Spot Sales. I went to school at New York University at night with the G.I. Bill paying for it. It made my two years in the Army during the Vietnam War worthwhile. Fortunately, my stint in the army was at Fort Hood, Texas.

Anita and I enjoyed our time together, but my life was complicated. My daughter, Debbie, and I were spending less time together. I felt terrible about that. However, we had to get accustomed to that. It was one of the most painful times of my life. My mother, who was always challenging to get along with, was less sympathetic about my marriage, and we argued a lot. Debbie and Anita were two of the bright spots in my life.

Eventually, Anita told her parents about my marital status, and I had a child. That didn't go over well. They forbade her from seeing me, but we continued to date. All these factors put a strain on our relationship, so we decided to see other people.

My life had gotten to the point where I had enough of New York and needed a change of scenery. I asked my employer for a transfer to the San Francisco Federal Reserve Bank. As a young kid, I always wanted to live in Southern California because of the warm weather, the beaches, and the attractive lifestyle. I wasn't going there, but I felt San Francisco would be close enough. Having a job when I got to San Francisco would be an advantage. A female coworker I knew at the New York Fed transferred to the San Francisco Fed and liked her new job and home. That convinced me to move. It was a turning point in my life.

I drove cross-country, and it gave me lots of time to think about everything going on in my life. I kept questioning myself. *What the heck was I doing?* I thought about turning around and heading back to New York several times. It didn't help that as I drove, I kept hearing Glen Campbell's very popular *By the Time I Get to Phoenix* playing on the radio.

When I got to Denver, I stopped for the night. The following day, it was a raging blizzard outside, and it was the middle of April. The storm continued for three days. *Was this a deal-breaker?* I talked to Anita several times on the phone. Thank goodness the motel had a restaurant and bar, but I was still getting stir-crazy. When I tried to go out one night, I had to return to the motel because the visibility was zero. My ski equipment was with me; I thought I could get in some skiing when the storm moved out. It didn't take me long to find out that most ski areas were closed for the season.

Finally, the storm lifted, and I checked out. Driving was treacherous. When I got to I-80 in Wyoming, it was slow going with cars and tractor-trailers strewn everywhere. Snow was blowing onto the already icy road. I only got as far as Rawlins, Wyoming, and spent the night. There were young nubile teenage waitresses in the restaurant where I ate that night. I was amused because they were overly attentive and definitely on the make. But I was only interested in dinner, a good night's sleep, and an early start in the morning.

The next day, the drive got better, and the road kept improving. A couple of days later, I drove over the Bay Bridge into San Francisco.

The move turned out to be beneficial. For the first time in my life, I met people who had jobs that supported their dreams. Some dreams even took priority over their careers. My new acquaintances wrote books, made real estate investments, created computer software, painted, and many other exciting things.

One of my co-workers would go to art museums and take photographs of paintings he liked. Then, he would make slides and project them onto a canvas and re-create the image with his paint. He gave me one of his re-creations, a modern, colorful, geometric piece to hang on my wall. Another one of my new friends, who was writing her first novel, encouraged me to write when she found out I was interested in writing. I'm forever grateful to her for pushing me in that direction.

Anita and I kept in touch; we missed one another. Finally, she came to San Francisco for a visit. She was more than ready to move out of the family home and strike out on her own. Anita asked, "What do you have to offer me if I move to California?"

I don't remember my response, but whatever I told her must have worked. She didn't move to San Francisco but to Hollywood, where she shared an apartment with her friend, Janet Bart, from New York. We were still apart, but it was cheap to fly back and forth between San Francisco and Los Angeles (about twenty-nine dollars round trip on PSA). That's how we spent weekends together.

Eventually, we wanted to spend more time with each other, and airfares kept going up, so I decided to move to Hollywood. We found a furnished penthouse apartment overlooking the pool with two lovely balconies on the top floor of a mid-century building. On a few clear days, you could see the Pacific Ocean. Our patios got a lot of afternoon sun. We planted a box garden where we grew herbs and tomatoes in one of them. Our rent was one-hundred twenty-five dollars a month. Where have those days gone?

When my divorce became final, I was still *persona non grata* with Anita's parents. One summer, Anita's mom and aunt came for a visit, and they stayed at a nearby hotel. But paranoid Anita had me move most of my stuff to our friend Janet's apartment up the street. I stayed away when her mom and aunt visited our apartment. The following year Anita's mom planned to come out again. We were on a ski trip to Mammoth. While riding a chairlift, the conversation went something like this: "What are we doing?" Anita asked.

"All I know is I'm not moving my stuff again."

"Well, what are we going to do?" she persisted.

"Let's get married. It's only a piece of paper."

After a long silence, I said, "If you want to get married, let's get married." Looking back, it wasn't very romantic, but that's how we ended up married.

The wedding was on the Friday evening of Memorial Day Weekend in 1975. We had the ceremony at a church on Hollywood Boulevard, which eventually became the Screen Actors' Guild headquarters for several years. (Years later, I volunteered at SAG, helping make appointments for actors to have their tax returns prepared by volunteers for free. I remember looking down with fond memories into what was the chapel where I had been married a few years earlier.)

One of the band members of Hamilton, Joe Frank, and Reynolds played the organ for our wedding. Janet Bart worked in the music business and arranged for him to be there.

There was a small reception at our apartment with several friends in attendance. We had two wedding cakes because Janet bought one and a guest brought another one. Following that, we honeymooned in Palm Springs that weekend. The weather was in the low one-hundreds. Anita couldn't take the heat and stayed in our motel room watching the movie *Meet Me in Saint Louis* on the TV. Every time I came in from the pool to cool off a little in the air conditioning, the film was still playing. It was on all afternoon because there were commercials every ten minutes. We still laugh about that trip and didn't return to Palm Springs for at least a decade after that.

Anita's mom never came out that summer. She had to plan our Brooklyn wedding. That second one happened in August, and we had a big wedding reception. The Top Hats provided the music. Anita's sister had her first son, and her father had forgiven her and accepted his other son-in-law, Joe Cannella. All was well in the Cannarili family. Her mother was relieved she didn't have to sneak around to see her older daughter anymore, and she was happy her younger one was married too. My parents loved Anita and were delighted about our marriage.

Anita got a permanent position at CBS as secretary to Michael Sevareid, son of the famous newscaster Eric Sevareid. When Anita started working for him, Michael was the CBS executive in charge of *All in the Family*, *MASH*, *One Day at a Time*, and several other popular sitcoms. It was a Golden Age for television. Those were the Fred Silverman days. The TV executive, Silverman, had his finger on the pulse of the American viewing public with multiple hit shows.

One night, Anita came home from work and said, "We're going to a party at Jim Nabors' house." A couple of New York producers were in town and met with Sevareid that day, and they extended an invitation to Anita. His house was in Bel Air, and Nabors was funny, friendly, and hospitable. He was happy to take us on a tour of his mansion. I couldn't believe we met Gomer Pyle, and he was such a nice guy. He was the first celebrity I met in Hollywood.

I was in my early thirties and continued to work in IT. After moving to L.A., I got a job at Computer Sciences Corporation. However, the work left me burned out. I started writing my first novel, which eventually became *Railway Avenue*.

I took a class at U.C.L.A. that explored the many avenues a writer could pursue. The instructor talked about writing fiction, non-fiction, screenwriting, and technical writing to name a few. The professor told us that we were writers if we came to her class. I told Anita and my daughter Debbie (who was living with us at the time) that I was a writer. They questioned me, "You're a *writer*?" The instructor also said if you wanted to be a good writer, you needed to get involved in different things and have many different experiences. She suggested theatre, maybe even acting, which re-lit an old interest—wanting to be an actor as a child—but I had never pursued that dream.

OUR FIRST HOUSE

After the wedding, we continued to live in our furnished apartment. We loved it, and the swimming pool was a nice amenity. In New York, my parents had one of those above-ground pools, but it was nothing like our Hollywood pool. That was a real treat that we enjoyed. That's where my daughter and I met my first friend in L.A., Vince Ciacci, who lived on the second floor with his wife. Eventually, they separated, and Vince's new girlfriend moved in and became his second wife. We became good friends. Vince was a hairstylist, and he would cut my hair. We were both from New York and of Italian descent with a lot in common. Mainly, we compared mothers. We found our Italian mothers were very similar. They were great cooks, but they also gave you *agita* (indigestion) while you ate.

It wasn't too long after our wedding that we bought a four-poster bed that we liked. The building management removed the furnished bed to make way for our new one. However, it made our bedroom a little cramped. That's when we began to talk about buying a house. L.A. hadn't yet gone through the housing boom that eventually fell upon the city. In some areas, houses were still affordable. We started looking in the Fairfax district, where we liked the Spanish-style homes. We quickly realized we couldn't afford anything around there, but some of the houses in the Hollywood Hills were still in our price range. I always wanted to live in those hills. A friend from San Francisco encouraged me to pursue my dream. There was one house we liked but couldn't afford. It was Spanish-style on a quiet hillside street close to the Hollywood Bowl.

Next, we considered Laurel Canyon, a funky area between the city and the San Fernando Valley. It housed celebrities, musicians, and artists. One of our favorite houses was at the top of the canyon. We loved the house and its address, 2001. It was a cantilevered house; the garage and most of the house hung out over the canyon, and the supports showed their age which scared us off.

We eventually found a two-bedroom, one-and-a-half-bath townhouse on Wonderland Avenue. Instead of cantilevered, this one was built into the hill, and you looked up at most of the property. Anita wasn't crazy about it. She missed New York and still wasn't convinced she wanted to live in California. I felt the house had potential, and we made an offer. The seller was a woman who was a PBS News anchor on KCET, the L.A. PBS station. The purchase price we negotiated was fifty-seven thousand, five-hundred dollars, a real bargain compared to today's housing market.

Laurel Canyon was considered a brush area and fire-prone, making it difficult to get insurance, which delayed our closing. Prices in L.A. started their upward spiral that summer. The seller wanted to back out of the deal because the house's value rose by thousands of dollars while in escrow. Our State Farm agent helped us get the necessary insurance, and we closed on the place one-hundred-twenty days after signing a contract.

On this narrow canyon street, there were no sidewalks. We had a two-car garage under the house. After moving in, we learned how treacherous getting in and out of that garage could be.

The front door was up a flight of stairs at the side of the house. The stairs continued to the backyard gate. You entered the living room through the front door, and the living room had a vaulted ceiling. We also had a kitchen, half bath, and laundry room on that level. Upstairs, there were two bedrooms and a full bath. The back bedroom had a sliding door to a private patio and the sloping hillside. The house was a cozy little place. Our friend Vicki Barnes' father, Bob Reggiani, called it a love nest when he came to dinner with his wife, daughter, and Hank Miller, Vicki's boyfriend.

We had fun furnishing the place. We bought an oversized playpen couch for the living room and a butcher block table for dining, surrounded by bentwood chairs with cane seats. We made a makeshift table of cement blocks and wooden shelves to hold our stereo and vinyl record collection. I built shelves in the front corners of the living room about ten feet above the floor for our tall speakers. There was a big empty wall above the living room that we filled with the Italian flag colors: white, green, and red material stapled to artists' frames. The living room floor and stairs to the second floor had dark brown shag carpet, which was in style in those days. I spent a Labor Day weekend putting track lighting on the living room ceiling for additional light. The living room had tall windows with dark brown shutters, and the bedrooms had shutters too. Those two rooms had maroon carpeting.

In our bedroom, the four-poster bed and two dressers still felt cramped. We made round night tables for each side of the bed. In the back bedroom, which had a sliding door to the patio, we had a waterbed and a desk constructed from an old door placed across sawhorses. I used it for writing. Those were the days before home computers, but I had an IBM Selectric typewriter to write on.

Anita's parents came to visit us in our new home. I was no longer *persona non grata*. I was happy because I liked them and wanted them to like me. They took us to Sears and bought us a washer and dryer. Cosmo helped me paint the ceiling in the bedroom we slept in. The popcorn-covered ceiling soaked up paint like crazy when I tried using a roller. Anita's father had been a house painter, bought me stiff brushes, and showed me how to paint that ceiling with a brush. He said, "Make a box with the paint in a small square area until you feel it's all covered. Then start another box." The paint job soaked up six gallons of paint.

On the humorous side, Cosmo brought a collection of artificial birds he attached to thin sticks and hung them from the roof covering our patio. We didn't know what to think of it. They stayed there for a few years until I removed the patio roof to get more sun in the yard.

Anita grew to like the house and was getting used to living in L.A. For one thing, she had an easy commute down the hill to CBS Television City in Hollywood, where she worked. I had a much longer commute to El Segundo (near Los Angeles Airport), about a thirty-five-minute drive on a good day. Our new commutes were a pleasure after riding New York subways for many years.

Having a hill behind the house meant there was no grass to cut. That was an advantage, but the fire department would inspect the hillside every spring and leave a summons to clear the brush. It was an annoying task because we had to hire someone. I tried doing it myself, and it wasn't easy. Once, I even got a bad case of poison oak. We hired a struggling artist friend to clear it one year. While working up there, she dislodged some large rocks that tumbled down the hill and took out part of our neighbor's deck railing.

Every year it was a different story. Most of the workers spoke very little English. I tried to tell them what they had to do. Sometimes they followed my instructions, and many times they didn't. The fire department would come by afterward to see that the hill conformed to the hillside brush regulations. It was a good preventive measure because there were only a few fires while we lived there, and none of them were close to us.

Our neighbors were exciting and eccentric. Rich Bertram lived directly across the street. He was a rock and roll guitarist from Ohio. He rode a very loud Harley motorcycle. We grew to love Rich and always referred to him as the mayor of our street because he always had a handle on what was going on in the canyon.

Someone from the band The Turtles also lived a few doors down on Rich's side of the street. I never saw when they did it, but the guy had an old Packard automobile put up on the hill where his house was.

Graham Nash wrote the song *Our House* about the house where he lived with Joni Mitchell on Lookout Mountain Road, a street behind Wonderland. The actress Christina Applegate lived on that street, too. As a teenager, she played the lead in our friend Jurg Ebe's student film *Johnathan*. For the movie screening in Pasadena, Jurg asked if we could pick Christina up and bring her to the screening with us. She was a sweet young lady and wonderful in the movie.

We also had the Wonderland Elementary School a few doors down from us. Wonderland Avenue was in the news when the porno star John Holmes was involved in multiple murders in a house further up the street. It was over a drug deal gone bad. We had friends who lived only a few doors from the murder scene. Until the police arrived, our friends heard the moaning of the only surviving victim of the assault.

Jerry Brown, the California governor, had a home on another street up the hill. One night, police vehicles with sirens wailing screamed past our house, and helicopters circled overhead. They had spotted a prowler on the governor's property.

Many different people lived in the rental house next door. It was the same design as our house, with our doors facing each other. The people who lived there were always interesting. When we first moved in, a family with two teenage boys and a large German Shepard named Brandon lived there. He was old and feeble. One summer evening, when our windows were open, we heard THUD, THUD, THUD from next door, followed by a loud THUD. Then, we heard the woman say, "Brandon! Are you alright?" The dog had fallen down the stairs from the second floor.

For a time, some transvestites lived there. One night, the police came and raided the place and led a bunch of them away. We heard they were using the house for prostitution. They moved out right after that. Some very spiritual friends of Rich Bertram moved in. They were getting over the death of their teenage son. They said the house had a bad vibe, and she would burn lots of candles and incense. After those folks moved out, another one of Rich's friends rented the place. His name was Michael. We liked him a lot. He practiced Buddhism and had a little alter where he meditated. We could usually hear him chanting. He opened a Thai restaurant named Toi on Sunset Boulevard in Hollywood. He wasn't Thai; he was Caucasian. It was popular with delicious food. We frequented it often.

We had a lot of fun in that house. There were parties, good food, and lots of love. The whole time we lived there, the house's value continued to appreciate. Was it time to sell and buy something else?

MY FIRST ACTING CLASS

When I decided to take up acting, it didn't take long to find an acting class in Hollywood; it would be the first one in my life. Bill Kulak, a friend, was an actor and recommended Tony Barr's Film Acting Workshop. Besides his role as a teacher, Tony was the school's founder. Our friend had attended classes there, felt enthusiastic about their approach to acting, and he piqued my interest.

Tony Barr was a CBS executive who worked in the same department as Anita. He headed the development of television series, mini-series, and movies. As executive producer for the network, he supervised *Magnum P.I.* and *Simon & Simon*. Before being a TV executive, Barr was an actor in minor roles, usually playing gangsters and heavies.

They held the workshop on a small studio lot in Burbank. That first night, I remember walking through the dark lot to a building in the back. I had been on the lot before for a daytime event and again for an interview for the class, but it looked different at night. There were empty buildings and facades. I felt I was living out one of my life's fantasies.

As I continued walking, many questions came to mind. *Was this the beginning of a new life for me? Or would it be a futile attempt to find something new?* I fantasized about becoming a star. *What would the people in class be like?* I felt actors were different than me. They were people like Jimmy Stewart, Gregory Peck, and Cary Grant. I wasn't raised with confidence about how I looked and spoke. It wasn't only my parents' fault. The nuns in Catholic grammar school didn't instill a lot of self-confidence.

When I reached the small one-story building where they held classes, I paid a woman seventy-seven dollars for my first four weeks. That was it. I was committed. She introduced me to a classmate who told me, "It's a good class. You'll like it." He introduced me to some of the other students, and others came up to me and introduced themselves. All of them were more interesting than most of the people I worked with, and that's why I wanted to make a career change; maybe acting would be the incentive I needed.

That night, everyone was excited because Tony would be teaching the class and not the other instructor. Tony welcomed me and introduced me to the group. Following that, he said, for my benefit, "I was typecast as an actor. I want to help actors learn techniques that will help you not get typecast as I did." Tony did look like a gangster. He was tall and skinny with deep-set eyes and heavy bags under them, and his hair was salt and pepper, but his voice was soft and pleasant when he spoke.

The curriculum I signed up for consisted of two classes. One was a scene study class, and the other was film acting. Tony Barr taught scene study; the other instructor led the film class.

I also met another student, an attorney, who felt learning some acting techniques would help him have a greater presence when he represented clients in court. That was interesting. I also talked to a guy that managed Dr. Joyce Brothers' career. She was a famous TV psychologist. He was there trying to understand the business from an actor/performer's point of view.

I had no acting experience and no preconceived ideas about acting. Barr said, "Acting is listening to the other actor, experiencing what the other actor says or does, and reacting." That made sense to me. When it came time for my partner and me to do the scene Tony assigned, he said, "Just be yourself."

The woman I was working with and I sat across a table, looked at each other, and tried to connect. She had a pleasant face with freckles and wore glasses. I was introverted, but acting felt natural to me, and I felt comfortable doing it with her. I thought she was a good actress, and I was happy to work with her. I wondered if she knew this was my first performance. Surprisingly, I wasn't nervous, but I wasn't talking naturally. I was acting, as Tony would soon point out.

The scene came from a TV detective show. I remember a line where I said, "The suspect was brandishing a nickel-plated revolver...." Tony stopped us at some point and said to me, "Slow down. Take your time. React to her before you look at your page for the next line. Stop acting. Now, start over again and just talk to her."

We did the scene a second time and got to the end. Barr gave me a few notes and said, "Come back with the scene memorized next week." I liked how he took his time with everyone, and we all performed a scene before the class ended.

I got to do the scene again the following week. Then eventually, I would do it on camera. After that first night, I was certain acting would bring out a part of me that I suppressed most of my adult life. "It's good therapy. That's what it is," one of the girls told me while we were on a break. What I enjoyed about acting was the thrill of creating and being someone else. Workshops like Tony's allowed you to experiment with different characters and situations.

At the end of the evening, I walked to the parking lot with a classmate. He seemed very spiritual and spoke about his life, God, and the East Coast, where he was also from. I told him a little about myself. We said goodnight. On the way home, I was still high from the evening, and for the first time, I started to believe that I could be an actor.

The film acting class was two days later. I don't remember much about the instructor other than his personality, which could be abrasive. That class was set up like a small studio with video cameras. We did scenes, recorded them, and watched and critiqued them at the end of the evening. I had heard my voice on tape before, but I listened to my voice and saw my image on video. It was a little disconcerting.

One night in the film acting class, we did a fun news show. We got to play news anchors and weather forecasters. The funny part of the scene occurred when one of the anchors sat on a whoopie cushion and reacted with a shocked look. Each actor who sat on the cushion had a different reaction.

I also enjoyed learning how to operate a video camera. Over time, one thing that stuck with me was "to lead the look." In other words, the image in the camera would not be in the center, but the person would have more space in front of them. That was helpful information whether you were a camera operator or an actor. We also learned about finding your light. If another actor blocked your light, we were instructed to make an adjustment and step into the light. Vice versa, we also talked about how not to block another actor's light.

We also learned about two-shots, over-the-shoulder shots, and rack focus. One of my favorite camera moves is rack focus, a very cool visual technique. The camera captures a close image, and by re-focusing, the image shifts to something in the background. Or, it could be something distant that becomes prominent. These were all valuable techniques to understand as a working actor.

I stayed in the class for several months and built my confidence, but I still felt like something was missing. I needed more tools and more training. I didn't know it at the time, but besides learning the skills I needed, acting classes helped keep my instrument (sometimes actors refer to themselves as an instrument) in tune, especially when acting jobs were few-and-far-between. There would be more classes for me in the future.

SYD FIELD & SHERWOOD OAKS EXPERIMENTAL COLLEGE

Syd Field was an early writing mentor of mine. He wrote the ever-popular book *Screenplay*. Published in 1979, it was the definitive book on screenwriting. It opened the door for other books about screenplays by other authors.

I met Field at the Sherwood Oaks Experimental College in Hollywood. Its second-floor space in a building on Hollywood Boulevard and Ivar Street had a warehouse feel.

Gary Shusett co-founded the school. (His brother Ronald co-wrote the *Alien* screenplay with Dan O'Bannon.) The school wasn't accredited, nor did it resemble how a real college operated. It was a trade school for the entertainment industry. Professional writers, producers, directors, and actors taught classes. Even the great Lucille Ball taught comedy acting classes for a while.

I attended a weekend-long screenwriting conference with industry professionals. Among the notable speakers were Buck Henry (*The Graduate*), John Melius (*Dirty Harry*, *Apocalypse Now*), Ernest Lehman (*North by Northwest*, *West Side Story*), Marshall Brickman (co-writer of *Annie Hall* with

Woody Allen), Syd Field, and many more. They all shared stories about projects they had worked on and their difficulties bringing them to fruition. I was learning that it wasn't an easy business to break into. I didn't want to get disillusioned and tried to stay positive. Syd Field was the bright light that got me through the negativity.

Syd was writing his first book when I met him. When the book was published, reading it was like sitting in the classroom listening to Syd. He was a terrific lecturer. His premise for explaining successful movies he called "the paradigm." He defined that as a three-act structure. Act 1 of the screenplay is the setup around thirty pages (approximately thirty minutes of screen time, about one minute per page.) The first ten pages usually contain the hook that pulls you into the story, an incident or event that propels the story forward. Around those first thirty pages, a plot point occurs. This incident or event sends the story in a different direction. One of the examples Syd used was the movie *Rocky*. He would say, "Rocky was a down-and-out fighter who gets his shot at the world championship." Act 2 is the confrontation that shows Rocky getting into shape to fight the champ. In Act 2, at about ninety pages into the story, the final plot point occurs, which drives the story to its conclusion. In act 3, the last act, Rocky fights the champion, Apollo Creed.

Wow! That made sense to me. It was the information I needed to write a screenplay. I could put it to work on the script I was writing.

Syd acquired his knowledge about screenplay structure in the Hollywood trenches, first as a reader for the David L. Wolper Company and later for Cinemobile. He claimed to have read hundreds of screenplays and concluded that most successful pictures contained the paradigm. Many writers of box office successes had been writing their scripts that way all along. Syd's book clarified this, thus introducing the paradigm to the rest of the world.

At the conference and in his class, Syd said, "People in this town will tell you about the roles they're going to play, the movies they're going to produce, and screenplays they're going to write." Syd went on to say, "If you have a screenplay in your hands that you wrote—you have more than most people in Hollywood." That made me feel good.

After listening to Syd at the conference, I was inspired to learn more and joined his screenwriting workshop. There were only a few students, so it was very personal, and Syd took a serious interest in our work. We had a good class of budding screenwriters who were already writing their screenplays when we joined Syd's class. He wanted us to have a completed first act by the end of the eight-week session. To help us get there, Syd would give us sections of *Screenplay*, which he was still writing. He wanted us to read it to see if what he wrote made sense to us or not and if it helped our writing. I felt it was an honor to contribute to his efforts.

We had a very enthusiastic and inspired group of writers who exceeded Syd's expectations. Many of us finished our first act before the session ended. One writer completed his screenplay. It was about the Detroit riots of the 1960s as seen through the eyes of hippies ingesting drugs. Despite the seriousness of the riots, it was hilariously funny. I don't know whatever happened to him or his script.

I worked on my first screenplay entitled *D.E.B.E.* in the class. It was about the introduction of robots into our daily lives. The title is an acronym for "does everything but eat," pronounced "Debbie." When an earthquake hits L.A. in the middle of the night, the robots escape into the neighboring community, and one of them falls into the wrong hands.

I took another eight weeks with Syd and completed the *D.E.B.E.* screenplay. I never sold it, but I had a finished script. As Syd had said, that was more than most people in Hollywood had. Unfortunately, I didn't stay in touch with the other writers in the class, so I don't know whether they were successful. After that, I never saw Syd again but was thrilled about the success of his first book. He taught all over the world, and the book became a bestseller. Someone in France plagiarized it, resulting in a lawsuit that ended in Syd's favor. Syd also authored other popular books about screenwriting and movies. If you are a budding screenwriter, I highly recommend Syd's book, *Screenplay*, and his subsequent books.

In the Colorado Rockies many years later, I met and became friends with a gentleman named David Rose, a raconteur. David grew up in Hollywood and had relatives in the movie business. One day, we talked, and he told me, "My cousin wrote a book about screenwriting."

I looked surprised and asked, "Syd Field?"

He was equally surprised and said, "Yes. How did you know?"

I related to him my experiences and relationship with Syd.

David went on to tell me about his now-famous cousin and his other relatives in the business.

When I transitioned to writing books many years later, I completed my second book, a memoir entitled, *Almost A Wiseguy*, about my friend Vince Ciacci's chilling life. Since that last class with Syd, I have thought about him often over the years. I wanted to tell him about my novel, *Railway Avenue,* and the fellowship I won for my screenplay, *Big White Bonneville*. I hoped I could entice him to read the "...Wiseguy" book and maybe write a blurb or review.

I Googled him and found his website, which had his email address. I sent him an email. Several days later, I received a response from one of Syd's cousins. Since I mentioned in my email that I was a friend of his cousin, David Rose, the cousin that wrote me said that Syd had just passed away. That cousin was trying to get a hold of David but didn't know how to reach him. I called David and relayed the bad news. I was sad to hear about Syd. I was sorry I hadn't stayed in touch with him. It reunited David with his family. He often talks to Aviva, Syd's widow. She's developing a documentary about Syd's life and has interviewed David for the project and wants to interview me since I was one of his early students.

Besides the paradigm, Syd suggested writing an outline before putting your story into screenplay format. It is a starting point even if your screenplay doesn't stick to your outline. He also said, "Write character biographies for all your main characters." I already learned to do that as an actor when playing a character. Syd said, "If you feel your script is eighty-five percent there, let it go." In other words, get it out to people who might be interested in it and move on to your next writing project. The paradigm, outlines, and character biographies are something I have found useful when writing novels and memoirs as well.

In the next chapter, Anita will tell you what was going on in her life.

ANITA'S EPIPHANY

Bob wanted to change his career, which made me think about my ambitions. I was still working at CBS as Michael Sevareid's secretary when he was promoted to Director of Miniseries. We moved from CBS Television City in Hollywood to new offices over the hill at CBS Studio City. From our house in Laurel Canyon, my commute was in the opposite direction and closer to home.

In Michael's new position, there was an opening for an assistant; I wanted the job. He felt I didn't have the necessary experience and opted for Jane Rosenthal, who later became Robert De Nero's partner in Tribeca Productions. Michael knew her from his time in New York when he was an actor in his twenties. He also acted in Hollywood. One of his notable roles was opposite Richard Burton in *Raid on Rommel*.

I felt slighted when I couldn't get the assistant position and saw the writing on the wall. I didn't want to spend the rest of my life working as a secretary. I was ambitious, and I knew I was capable of much more. I didn't have a college degree because my mother told me to be a secretary. That was the best job. Sevareid's refusal to promote me motivated me, and I was determined to do something creative in the entertainment industry.

When I initially took the job at CBS, Sevareid's secretary, Rosemary Hansen, trained me, and we became friends. Rosemary left CBS to work at her husband's new production company, Ed Hansen and Associates. Ed had a background in Chicago advertising. Hansen's new company did commercials and documentaries. Rosemary and I kept in touch. One day over lunch, she said, "I want to stop working. Why don't you replace me as secretary for Ed?"

It was another secretarial job, but I insisted, "I'll take it only if I can work on productions." I took the job and gave up the usual benefits a corporate position provided. Fortunately, Bob was still working at Computer Sciences Corporation, and his medical insurance covered us. My new job was on Sunset Boulevard in Hollywood, a bit further commute than Studio City but an easy commute.

I was still doing office work, but I began to work on productions as a production assistant and script supervisor. I was detail-oriented and enjoyed what I was doing.

A filmmaker we knew had worked for Warren Miller, the famous ski film producer-director. Our friend said Miller didn't pay well, but the dinners were fabulous. I don't know for sure that this is true. However, that was true for Ed Hansen as well. He was a wine connoisseur, and there were many dinners and parties with delicious food and expensive wines.

I got Bob to work on the crew for a commercial we were doing for the Houston Lumber Company in the Palm Springs area. He also had an on-camera appearance alongside the talent in the commercial, Don Drysdale, the famous Dodger pitching ace and Hall of Famer. Bob said, "Even though I'm a Yankee fan, working with Don Drysdale is exciting. My Uncle Dan grew up in Brooklyn and was a lifetime Dodger fan. When I was a kid, we would harass each other every World Series when the Dodgers and Yankees played. He'd be impressed I was in the commercial with the famous pitcher."

As time went on, I got more involved in the productions and spent less time in the office. One summer, I was out of the office working on a production while my mom, sister, and nephews came from Florida for a visit. My sister Mary filled in for me at the office, answering the phones and typing. She enjoyed her short stint working in Hollywood. The production work inspired me to go back to school. At first, I went to Sherwood Oaks Experimental College and took a filmmaking class where we shot a short film over a weekend.

I enjoyed working on the Ed Hansen produced film for Mohamed Ali's retirement, in which they encapsulated clips from his career. Ali and his entourage would come up to the office, and he would playfully spar with Hansen. As a result of the project, we attended the retirement party for Ali at the Los Angeles Forum. In exchange for that project and some others, Jerry Buss, the owner of the Forum, paid Hansen with tickets to some of the shows at the venue. Bob and I saw Rod Stewart; Earth, Wind and Fire; the Lippizan Stallions; and several other shows.

Ed Hansen and Associates also had the girl band the Go-Go's as clients and produced some projects with them. We did a motorcycle documentary about California's Owens Valley. Ed also got the California State Fair in Sacramento as a client for several years. I worked on that too.

Ed Hansen's significant successes were his mostly nudie films with the bosomy stripper Kitten Natividad. I think that the first one, *Takin' It Off,* was financed by suspicious money. There were a lot of shady-looking characters hanging around the outdoor set. And a helicopter kept circling above to see the naked women. My co-worker Bob Canning and Ed Hansen co-wrote the script.

That movie was a windfall for the company and led to a series of similar films that kept them in business. On the internet, they describe Ed Hansen as a "nudie producer/director," but before those exotic movies, he had won awards for some of his documentaries and commercials.

When Bob was a more experienced actor, he got a part in one of the Ed Hansen films entitled *Party Plane*. He played the first frequent flyer program member for a down-and-out airline that saved itself from bankruptcy when the young, attractive female flight attendants started stripping on board.

As projects began to dry up for Ed Hansen and Associates, so did paychecks which came less frequently. My co-worker, Ann Hyatt, resigned to take a production job at the Playboy Channel.

Bob will tell you about his photographers in the next chapter.

BOB'S PHOTOGRAPHERS

I quickly learned that good pictures are one of an actor's most important things. Your pictures and resume are your calling card. A good photo got you in the door for casting purposes. Typically, this was a headshot (a close-up of your head) that you can submit to agents, casting directors, producers, and directors. It had to be a clear picture that hopefully showed them that you looked like the character they were trying to cast. The worst thing that could happen is you walk in the door, and your picture(s) don't look like you.

I don't remember the name of the first photographer I used. I found him through an ad he ran in the trade paper *DramaLogue*. One of the things I remember about him was his two birds, a big white cockatoo and a little albino cockatiel who liked to walk around outside. The cockatoo sat on a wooden replica of a biplane that hung from the photographer's ceiling. Anita saw them too, and we fell in love with the cockatiel and thought about getting one someday.

For the photoshoot, we took pictures outdoors in his neighborhood. He told me to bring a few costume changes. While he photographed me, he asked me to smile, frown, look angry, and other facial expressions. I changed into the different outfits that I had brought.

In those days, black and white photos were the standard. It took a few days before the contact or proof sheets were ready. This was a single sheet of eight by ten-inch photographic paper that contained a set of mini prints the same size as the negative film frames. It provided a simple way to review and select the final images to enlarge. We had a lot of nice pictures, which made it harder to decide which to use.

First, I had to pick the ones I liked, and then for a better image, they needed cropping. You cropped photos using a crayon on the contact sheet to mark how you wanted the final printed image to look. The photographer took care of getting the eight by tens back to you. Once you had them, you could take them to various labs around town. They would reproduce mass quantities—maybe a hundred or two-hundred copies to give to your agent, manager, or for your submissions. The process was costly from beginning to end, an expense that the unemployed actor had to foot.

Those first pictures opened a few doors for me. But no matter how many good shots you had, you always seemed to need new ones because you change over time, people got tired of seeing your same old photos, or they weren't getting you through doors anymore. Anita was a pretty good photographer, so she took some pictures of me. We had a great relaxed rapport and got several good shots. In one, I had a head full of curly black hair. It gave me a sinister, crazed look. We liked that one, and I had a lot of success with it. It got me auditions and some work.

A few years later, an actress friend had some interesting pictures. She recommended her photographer, Martin—he went by the one name. He was Hungarian, spoke with a heavy accent, wore thick-lensed glasses, and was funny. It wasn't hard to crack a smile with Martin. He made me laugh all the time. When he talked, tiny droplets spewed out of his mouth. I tried to stay a safe distance away.

On the walls in the lobby of his Sunset Boulevard studio, he had large prints of famous actors, male and female, that he had photographed over the years. What stood out most about Martin's work were the subject's eyes. He had a way of capturing the essence of their character through their eyes. His lighting was unique with dark shadows, and his prints had a sepia tone to them. Once I met and worked with Martin, I never looked for another photographer.

When I first started working with him, it was at his Sunset Boulevard Studio. He was aging, and I don't think he had the volume of business anymore to warrant the high rent of Sunset Boulevard, so he moved his studio to his condominium a few blocks away.

I was always satisfied with his photos. He even took some professional-looking pictures of Anita.

MY EARLY ACTING WORK

Now I had some training, had my pictures, and wanted to work. Every week when *DramaLogue* came out, I would scour the casting notices for roles I could submit for. My new photos worked because I got an audition for the three-character one-act play *The Shirt* by Leonard Melfi and was cast in the role of Marcy. It was about a black and white couple befriended by a Southern gentleman. He invites them to his hotel room, where he puts on a loud Hawaiian shirt, and a terrifying transformation occurs.

It was my first acting job and first death scene. I was thrilled about getting the part and enjoyed working on the production. The director did a good job bringing the play to fruition. We had a run at the Hollywood Actors' Theatre. It was a small forty or fifty-seat theatre, and attendance was sparse. There was no pay. In most of the theatre productions in L.A., the actors weren't paid. There was pay if you were in a play under the jurisdiction of the stage actors' union, Actor's Equity, and you were a member of that union. In Hollywood, most of those jobs went to well-established actors. People did plays in Hollywood for the experience. It might also result in a TV or movie role.

Several years later, I got to reprise my role as Marcy in another production of *The Shirt* in a lovely little theatre in Pasadena of about fifty seats. I remembered some of the lines from that first production for the audition. I got the part, and I was anxious to see how much I had grown as an actor. I felt much more confident and enjoyed doing it again.

Another one-act play, *Open 24 Hours'*, was on the same bill. I met and became friends with Andrew Piecka. He was in *Open 24 Hours'*. I also played a bum in that play.

The Shirt was up first. In one of our performances, something happened—somebody said a line that propelled us to the end of the play. There was no way to go back. The antagonist had to kill the woman who played my girlfriend and me. The play ended ten minutes early. I'll never forget the shocked look on Andrew's face when the three of us walked into the dressing room following the audience's applause. Andrew was still applying his makeup, and the other characters didn't have on makeup or costumes. They had to get ready quickly during the intermission.

Talk about learning experiences. That was a great one that showed that you never know what will happen in live theatre. This production had a much better turnout than the first one I did.

Besides theatre, there were many film student projects with casting notices in *DramaLogue*. Student filmmakers from U.S.C., U.C.L.A., Columbia College, American Film Institute (AFI), and other local film schools were always casting something. I started auditioning for them.

One of the first parts I won was a U.S.C. student film about a futuristic time when the government could watch you through your TV set. I enjoyed working on it and had some nice scenes. There was no pay in these films either. You did them for the experience and got a copy for your demo reel. You never knew if one of these budding filmmakers would strike it big in Hollywood and remember you for a part. The work was the same as working on a professional production; however, the students were also learning at your expense.

Then, I got a role in a Columbia College film in which I was with friends on a camping trip cut short by a serial ax murderer who chops off our heads. Hey, it was work, and I was practicing my craft.

One night, we were filming behind the school, and we heard a man with a raspy voice say, "Whatta you guys doing?" It was the comedian Red Foxx whose offices were next door. He was peeking over the wall that separated the two buildings.

I got my first paying job through a casting notice in *DramaLogue*. It was a non-union training film for correction officers. I played an out-of-control prisoner who takes a guard hostage with the sharpened end of a toothbrush pressed against his jugular vein. The lesson for correctional officers was how to deescalate that type of situation. We filmed it at the old Los Angeles County jail. It was no longer a county jail, but they used it for movies and TV productions. It was the same place that had held the Manson Clan and Sirhan Sirhan, the murderer of the presidential candidate, Bobby Kennedy. Being there felt a little creepy, which helped feed my craziness. The people were pleasant to work for, and I received my first acting paycheck and a copy of the film.

MAGIC CASTLE & TENNIS

While Anita worked for Michael Sevareid, she met a writer/producer named Jeff Segal, who pitched movie ideas to her boss. Jeff was short, thin with a head full of blond hair, and wore wire-rimmed glasses. He was quick-witted, funny, and ambitious. He wrote screenplays and wanted to be a producer. It was the beginning of a long, fun relationship.

Anita told Jeff we were avid tennis players, and he invited us to play in his Fourth of July tennis tournament. A few people Anita worked with at CBS showed up for the match. Bill Kulak was one of them. He was one of the people we usually played tennis with every week.

That day, we met some of Jeff's friends. There was a fellow named Lawrence. He was Jeff's closest friend and confidant. I believe they knew each other from a previous business they had been in. Lawrence, an eccentric germaphobe, was in his thirties and drove a Rolls Royce. Jeff said, "Lawrence made a fortune in puka shells when they became popular in the 1970s."

That evening, there was an award party in Buck and Margaret Kartalian's backyard in the San Fernando Valley. They were good friends of Jeff, who played in the tournament that day. Buck was a professional wrestler and character actor. He was short, muscular, and very funny. He had an extensive list of credits. As a young actor, Buck was in the movie *Mr. Roberts*. One night, we watched an old rerun of a Dean Martin and Jerry Lewis variety show, and Buck was cavorting with the comedy team. His wife Margaret was short, wore glasses, and was a housewife, mother, and a craft person. This Armenian couple was in their forties and fun to be around. In the tournament, the winning players won awards. The party ended with fireworks.

Margaret and Buck were yearly participants at the Renaissance Faire held in a wooded area in Agora, California. Margaret usually sold her craft pieces, and Buck performed a show with feats of strength. Seeing them was always fun. One of my favorite things about the fair was the large, barbequed beef rib that must have been about a foot long.

Jeff was also a magician, which enabled him to become a famed Hollywood Magic Castle member. We spent many fun nights at the castle on a hill above Hollywood Boulevard. Jeff gleefully took his guests on a tour of the place. The Magic Castle was full of surprises that started in the downstairs bar with two fun features. One was Irma, the invisible piano player. You could request just about any song or musical piece, and Irma would play it. However, all you saw were the piano keys moving. Another fun thing was the bar stool near the piano; it slowly went down when someone sat on it. If you were the victim, your chin was even with the bar top and still descending before you realized what was happening.

From the bar, we went upstairs to the various showrooms where professional magicians performed various feats of magic, from card tricks to people disappearing and bodies cut in half. Sometimes, we just had drinks, and sometimes we went for dinner and the shows. The food was always delicious. The Kartalians were usually there, Jeff and Lawrence, and one or two other guests.

Halloween at the Castle was always fun—the costumes were exceptional. One year, Buck dressed as a woman, and under his dress, which he lifted to shock people, he had a huge stuffed penis that Margaret made for him. They called it "a *juuje.*"

Jeff mentioned on several occasions, "We have to attend the séance dinner sometime." He showed us the private room where they held it. As promised, we had seven or eight people one night and went to the séance with its five-course dinner. Jeff knew the actor, Jon Voight, and invited him and his girlfriend, Marcheline Bertrand. She's Angelina Jolie's mother. Voight and Bertrand were both friendly and comfortable to be with.

Dinner was delicious, and the séance followed. To be honest, it was a hokey affair. Lights would go on and off, doors and cabinets would open and slam shut, voices from the dark would materialize, and metal shackles mysteriously appeared on the table. We all agreed it was fun but had no plans to attend again.

Being a screenwriter, Jeff loved movies, and many times we went out to dinner followed by a movie. One particular movie I remember going to with Jeff was the maligned Michael Cimino movie *Heaven's Gate.* We all enjoyed the expansive setting and story. We couldn't fathom the film's bad reviews. It was also panned for its long length and cost overruns.

It's funny how you can hang around with people for so long, and then one day, you stop doing that. Jeff became a producer at the animation house of Hanna-Barbera. Occasionally, we would see Margaret and Buck. I don't know what happened to Jeff, but the times we spent together were special. I will hold them in my heart forever.

Anita and I continued to play tennis at least twice a week. We usually had a steady Sunday morning doubles match. Sometimes it was mixed doubles with a man and woman on one side and the same on the other. Many times, it would be three guys and Anita. She became a pretty good player because she played with men and could beat most women in singles.

When Jeff Siegal's Fourth of July tournaments stopped, Anita and I organized one several years later. We had quite a few people show up. A Swedish guy Anita knew was a ringer. He beat everyone—even some of our friends who were top players. The award party was in our backyard in Laurel Canyon. The evening ended with the remaining guests watching the Fourth of July fireworks celebration from New York on TV.

MY FIRST TV MOVIE

I registered with a casting company that filled background positions. They had put me to work on several projects in movies and commercials. One day, they called about a part in a TV movie of the week entitled *Evita Peron*, starring Academy Award Winner Faye Dunaway as Evita. I was excited about the job, which consisted of several days of work. It was my first movie of the week. I played one of Evita's assistants and had several scenes with Dunaway. We shared a moment in one scene; I was surprised when she squeezed my hand. Another day, I was in Evita's death scene. She wasn't in bed for the shot (it was from her point of view); the camera operator sat on the bed, shooting our reactions with his camera.

They used to say that Faye Dunaway was difficult to work with, but she was very nice to me. The director was the famous, award-winning Marvin Chomsky (*Holocaust*). The Evita movie had an extensive cast and big-name actors such as James Farentino (I was in several scenes with him), Michael Constantine, Rita Moreno, Jose Ferrer, and Bill Baldwin. I never felt intimidated by their star power. I wasn't star-struck either and enjoyed every moment of it.

I worked several days in different scenes at Raleigh Studios on Melrose Avenue in Hollywood, across from Paramount Studios. It was fun working on a period piece. We got to dress in clothes from the forties and fifties. (Studio wardrobe departments have extensive collections of clothing.) I remember wearing expensive silk dress shirts, ties, and fine wool suits.

One day when I was sitting in a quiet spot outside the studio set, Dunaway came off the sound stage and turned to go to her dressing room. She passed me, stopped, turned around, and said, "Hello!" I did one of those stupid comedy double takes and turned around, thinking she was talking to someone else—but she was talking to me.

I was surprised and said, "Oh! Hi! Nice to see you." We smiled at each other, and she walked off to her dressing room.

A couple of years later, I got a call to work on a movie in Bel Air. It was another period piece, and I was standing in a line of guys waiting to get a 1940s-style haircut. We were behind a Bel-Air mansion where they parked makeup trucks and dressing-room trailers. Suddenly, Faye Dunaway came out of the house and walked past us. She stopped, turned, looked in my direction, and said, "It's nice to see you again." Yes, I did it again—the stupid double take. I don't even remember what I said. I must have mumbled something. Nevertheless, the guys standing in line with me were impressed and quizzed me after Faye went into her trailer.

The movie was *Mommie Dearest*, the true-life story of Joan Crawford with Dunaway as Crawford and directed by Frank Perry (*David and Lisa*, *The Swimmer*). I got several days' work. Some of them were on the Paramount lot. It was my first time there, and I got to eat lunch at the commissary. I was thrilled to eat in a studio commissary, and it was also a first for me. Mike Connors, who played *Mannix*, a detective on TV, was eating several tables away. After that, I always thought Paramount had the best commissary, and it was my favorite studio with its back lot of old building facades. I wasn't a member of the Screen Actors Guild, but I was paid SAG scale for that movie.

It was my first feature film. Anita and I went to one of the big theatres in Westwood to see the movie when it came out. One of the scenes I appeared in was outside Joan Crawford's house, the night she won her Oscar for *Mildred Pierce*. I played one of her devoted fans, and we kept saying, "We love you, Joan! We love you, Joan!"

They filmed one part of the scene at the Bel Air house. Several weeks later, the reverse angle of the scene was shot at Paramount Studios. Anita and I laughed so much when we saw me on that big screen. I must have been ten feet tall. People around us in the theatre probably wondered what we were laughing about. The movie was most famous for the hanger scene in which Joan screams at her children, "No more wire hangers!" Unfortunately, the film received unfavorable reviews, but it was an excellent experience.

Anita will tell you about going back to school in the next chapter.

ANITA GOES BACK TO SCHOOL

In 1979, I was still working at Ed Hansen & Associates and getting hands-on production experience, but I wanted to learn more about TV and film production. Someone told me about Columbia College in Hollywood, a trade school for TV and film students. The school's headquarters were in Chicago. I chose the Hollywood branch because it catered to working people who wanted to pursue their education at night. It was close to home and work and affordable, unlike other film schools in Los Angeles such as USC, U.C.L.A., and Loyola Marymount. So, I enrolled.

I had no college experience or credits, so I spent my first two years in the TV production track, which included the usual college-required academic curriculum: History, English, and other courses. There were also Acting Classes, TV productions, commercials, video editing, and more. I enjoyed most of the instructors, who were professionals from the entertainment industry, some my age, some younger than me, or not much older. I was older than one of my favorite instructors, Bruce A. Block. He was a film producer and consultant who had directed commercials, corporate films, and visual effects. He also produced

Father of the Bride, Father of the Bride II, and *The Parent Trap.*

At thirty-two years old, I was like a mother to my younger counterparts, some barely out of high school. They called me "Mom." I enjoyed my fellow students. They were an international bunch from Africa, Europe, Asia, the Middle East, Latin America, and a mix of American students whose parents were footing the bill for their education. For some of the international students, their home countries subsidized their education. With so many students from other countries, there were language barriers. However, their enthusiasm to create TV and film overcame those obstacles.

Like many college students, I had to take out student loans to pay for my education. My parents contributed some, and I continued working full-time. My young friends, whose parents paid for their schooling, were still too young to appreciate the value of their education and didn't have to work while going to school. I also had an advantage over my fellow students because I had already been working in the entertainment business, and I appreciated my education.

I attended classes five nights a week. It put a strain on our marriage. But Bob and I enjoyed collaborating, writing skits and short scenes for school productions that I directed, and Bob acted.

One of our first projects was a short piece called *Waiting for Woody.* It was about two actors waiting for an audition with Woody Allen, and they tormented each other with one-upmanship. Bob played an older actor, and he recruited a guy from one of his classes to play the other character. Of course, I was nervous and worried, but I received a favorable positive critique from my instructor and fellow students. That helped boost my confidence.

I also made a commercial, a Public Service Announcement (PSA). I called it *Super Pooling*; it encouraged people to carpool to work. There was a voice-over, and when the carpoolers arrived at their work location and got out of the car, they were *Star Wars* characters. I had a Darth Vader, Yoda, and Obi-Wan Kenobi. Bob was the driver dressed in a business suit, and there was a woman passenger dressed in business attire. Our friend, Steve Sansweet, who has the world's largest collections of Star Wars memorabilia, loaned us the Star Wars masks.

I breezed through those first two years, made the honor roll, and continued into the film production program with its two-year curriculum. I met other passionate students in the film program that I liked working with, and we shared the same interests. I worked on their productions, and they worked on mine.

One of my first assignments was to create a short slide show. The theme Bob and I came up with was a day in a Sunday newspaper's life. I shot photographs of Bob as the subject, dressed in a robe and gathering up his scattered Sunday L.A. Times in the morning. It continued with shots of reading the paper all day long and ended with him falling asleep at night with the newspaper spread across his chest. I set the whole thing to some comical music synced to the slide show. The project was well-received and boosted my confidence, which helped me move on in the program.

I sometimes came home with my fellow students to unwind during those days. It was always fun to hang out with them. Other nights, we went to Shakey's, a Hollywood pizza place and bar. Bob would join us sometimes. One night at Shakey's, the guys pulled a prank on a fellow student from South America. He wasn't a drinker, and they ordered him a Long Island Iced Tea, which wasn't a tea at all. It was a potent alcoholic drink that knocked the poor guy for a loop.

Those were exciting and creative times for Bob and me. It was a fun extension of our marriage and offered a glimpse of what our future could be like. I set my sights on producing and directing as a career goal.

In the next chapter, Bob will tell you about working in a Francis Ford Coppola movie.

BOB WORKS ON ONE FROM THE HEART

In 1982, I got my first Hollywood agent. He wasn't a top-tier agent, far from it, but he was someone who could get me work. His office was in a rundown section of Hollywood. Initially, I went there to give my screenplay *D.E.B.E.* to the agency's literary representative. He took it and said, "I'll read it. If it's any good, I'll shop it around."

He introduced me to the owner/theatrical agent when I told him I was an actor. The owner looked over my pictures and resume. He wasn't very friendly, but I thought that was probably how agents were. Then, he told me in a gruff voice, "Bring me some more pictures and resumes so I can start submitting you." Before I left his office, he said, "Go to Zoetrope and give them your picture and resume. They're looking for actors." As it turned out, that was a great suggestion. That day was a big win—my first literary and theatrical agent.

The literary agent read *D.E.B.E.* and submitted it to Zoetrope. The following week, he told me someone at the studio liked it. I want to think it was Frances Coppola who read it. Unfortunately, nothing else came of it.

I took the theatrical agent's advice and went to Zoetrope Studios in Hollywood. I met the casting director in the casting department, the lovely, friendly Elisabeth Leustig. (At the age of fifty, Ms. Leustig died in a Moscow traffic accident in 1995.) There were actors' pictures and resumes everywhere. It didn't look like mine would ever surface to be called for an audition or work. After a few weeks, and to my surprise, they did call me and cast me in Francis Coppola's latest project, *One from the Heart*. It was an impressive production. Based on his experiences with *Apocalypse Now*, Coppola didn't want to repeat his over-budget and production-plagued problems due to bad weather and other issues.

The setting for *One from the Heart* was Las Vegas. Coppola built the Vegas Strip in one of his studio's sound stages, complete with Vegas' bright neon lights. I was impressed and felt like I was in Las Vegas. It was a musical starring Nastassja Kinski, an up-and-coming starlet. Gene Kelly was the choreographer. What a thrill to see him up close. He moved with the grace of the great dancer that he was. When he walked across the sound stage, it appeared like he glided a few inches above it.

One of the other stars was Frederic Forrest, who made a name for himself as the New Orleans chef/soldier in *Apocalypse Now*. He was friendly and approachable; we shared a few words between takes during a bar scene.

I was a fan of Teri Garr, a very busy actress. We spent hours shooting a street scene in which we kept passing each other on the make-believe Vegas Strip. For hours, Coppola shot this scene from many angles.

At the curbside in one setup, I looked down. The award-winning cinematographer, Vittorio Storaro, operated a camera that stood on blocks at our feet with the camera aiming up at us.

Coppola did most of his directing from a silver Airstream trailer parked outside the sound stage. They were beginning to use video playback fed from the motion picture film camera. Coppola took advantage of this new technology to review scenes immediately. Previously, they had to develop the film before viewing it a day or two later in a screening room. Occasionally, Mr. Coppola would come out on the set and talk to his actors and crew. Sometimes, he would do it over the same loudspeaker he called "action" and "cut" from.

Despite the impressive cast and set, the movie bombed, but Coppola's touch was apparent in its look and feel. I must have wound up on the cutting room floor because I didn't see myself in the final version. Nevertheless, it was a thrill and a great experience. Unfortunately, the studio ran into financial difficulties, shut down, and I never worked on another Coppola film.

METHOD ACTING

In my quest to learn more about acting, I talked with other actors about the craft, read books, and researched acting classes. They taught several different techniques around town. I took an acting class at U.C.L.A., and the instructor talked about Method Acting. It derived from what Konstantin Stanislavski called "the System." In the early 1900s, the Moscow Art Theatre developed this revolutionary acting technique. I felt like I was missing something in my training. It tweaked my curiosity, and I wanted to know more about this approach to acting.

There are a lot of misconceptions about the Method. Because Marlon Brando mumbled his dialogue in *Streetcar Named Desire* and other movies, people bad-mouthed Method acting. But that's not it. It provides the actor with tools for preparing for a role or when a scene or character doesn't come easily. Through Method training and rehearsals, the actor learns to be honest in performances by understanding and experiencing a character's inner motivation and emotions. This acting technique gives the actor flexibility to experiment and helps overcome life's conditioning, acquired habits, and personal experiences to stimulate the imagination to portray a character's true feelings and reactions.

The Method became an American style of acting that was controversial and had a mystique about it. Lee Strasberg, the co-founder of the Actors Studio in New York, taught his interpretation of Stanislavski's System. The Actors Studio was initially called the Group Theatre. Its early members were Elia Kazan, Lee Strasberg, Harold Clurman, Cheryl Crawford, Robert Lewis, and Tennessee Williams. Strasberg and Kazan taught. The Studio was free to members who were either invited to join or had to audition for a place.

Stella Adler, a famous actress/teacher, questioned the usefulness of some of what Strasberg taught. The source of their disagreement was over Strasberg's use of what they called Affected Memory (or emotional recall). In Affected Memory, you use your senses to go into your past and re-create a situation that evokes emotions and sense memories to use in a scene. Adler felt the approach was unnecessary and torturous for actors.

After she had studied with Stanislavski in Paris, Adler taught her version of the Method. Stanislavski confirmed Adler's suspicions that Affective Memory was a technique he had abandoned. That proved what Adler had claimed all along. As per Stanislavski, Adler taught actors to behave realistically using their imaginations instead of emotional recall. She emphasized that actors needed to explore a character's situation and take actions appropriate to the circumstances. To develop this, she said, "Actors must consistently observe life, a task that requires discipline, visualization, and observation."

Many famous actors adapted the Method into their work, most notably Marlon Brando and Robert De Niro, who studied with Adler, while Al Pacino and Marilyn Monroe were proteges of Strasberg. These are only a few of the many actors who studied and used the techniques these two influential acting teachers taught.

I read some of Stanislavski's books but needed in-class experience to learn the exercises and other techniques. An actress friend that we played tennis with recommended Jenna McMahon's class. She taught it in her home in the Hollywood Hills, a few minutes from where I lived. Jenna was a comedy writer for the *Carol Burnett Show*. She had been a comedian, an actress, and an acting teacher. In New York, she studied acting under Stella Adler.

So, I joined McMahon's private class, but I got bored. All I did was exercises meant to improve my observational skills, and then there were the sensory exercises intended to develop your senses to use them realistically in scenes. Some of these dealt with intentions. For example, she would give you a situation like a reunion with a father you hadn't seen in years and how you would prepare for that meeting. Part of my problem with Jenna's class was that I was still too new to the craft to appreciate what she was teaching. Years later, I read in the trade paper *DramaLogue* that Stella Adler would be in town teaching a class on how to do a period piece. Curious about her, I signed up.

The most striking thing I remember was when Adler made her entrance, they told us to give her a standing ovation—and she expected it. Also in the class were John Ritter, Stockard Channing, and some other working actors I recognized but didn't know their names. We watched scenes from plays by Tennessee Williams, Arthur Miller, and other period pieces by famous playwrights. Adler was tough on the actors who performed and questioned how they prepared. She added inspiration and advice about techniques to dig into the period, its historical facts, mannerisms, and other considerations such as wardrobe and hairstyles.

It might seem odd, but she scolded the class about applauding with little enthusiasm. I can still hear her saying, "You must applaud as though you mean it!" It was a good lesson, and I still clap my hands with vigor whenever the occasion arises, and it reminds me of Ms. Adler.

After Jenna McMahon's class, I found another one run by two New York actors, Rick Sevy and Ray Cole, who were members of the Actors Studio, which also had a branch in Hollywood. Rick was very tall with a big frame. He wore thick-lensed black glasses. Ray was much shorter, handsome, Italian looking.

Rick taught the class I joined, and I started with sensory exercises. There are about twelve of them. As you advanced through the training, you added other things—movement, sounds, words, and monologues.

You started with the coffee cup exercise, which the actor created from his senses. There was no physical cup of coffee. You tried to feel the heat, the shape of the cup, the aromas coming from it, and more. Afterward, Rick would critique what he saw and tell you what to incorporate next time. Of course, you practiced them daily on your own.

Before the exercises, we worked on relaxing the body. Strasberg believed actors had to be relaxed on stage and in a film to do their best work. The key was finding tension and eliminating it through movement and sound.

I don't remember how long I was in the class, but Rick and Ray asked me to be in a play they were producing, and Ray directed. My work in class must have impressed them, and I didn't have to audition for the part. The play *If Men Played Cards Like Women Do* was a parody with four men playing cards and talking about their hats and other things women usually spoke about. It was an old and dated play, but we made it work. I was thrilled to be on stage with the other three very seasoned older actors. Sue Mengers, the famous Hollywood talent agent, came to the play. Sevy and Cole introduced me. I think they thought she might recognize my talent and want to represent me, but that never happened. At the time, I was naïve about who she was and took meeting her for granted, as I did with many of those early experiences.

After a while, we learned improvisation and how to use it in rehearsals, especially for finding the subtext (the thoughts underlining the scene's dialogue). We had a talented group of improvisational actors and put on improv shows at a basement theatre off of Sunset Boulevard. The theatre was so small that once you were backstage, you felt trapped; there was no back door. I enjoyed improvising. It came easily to me, and I was good at it, probably because I was a writer and could create dialogue and situations.

I would eventually move on from the class. The Lee Strasberg Theatre and Film Institute was around the corner from where Rick taught. As a result of his class,

I gained a much better understanding of the basics of the Method. I thought, *why not go right to the source.*

It was 1981 when I started taking classes at the Strasberg Institute. I had to go through an interview for acceptance. It was with the school's executive director. She said, "All of the teachers here have been personally trained by Mr. Strasberg before they can teach at the school." I'm still not sure what that meant. Did Strasberg have a particular class for training instructors? Most of the teachers were members of the Actors Studio. Was that membership enough to teach Strasberg's Method? The school had an impressive faculty of actors/teachers I had seen on television and in movies. Susan Peretz, who played Al Pacino's distressed wife in the movie *Dog Day Afternoon,* taught. Sally Kirkland also taught at the school. She won a Golden Globe, an Independent Spirit Award, and was nominated for the Academy Award for Best Actress in the movie *Anna* in 1987.

My interview went well, and the executive director welcomed me into the program. The classes were expensive, but I was making good money in the computer industry to afford them. The woman suggested two classes I would probably enjoy.

The first class was on Tuesday evening with Laurie Hull, Ph.D. Her daughter, Dianne Hull, was an accomplished actress that Lee Strasberg had taken under his wing as a young girl. Dr. Hull's class was for actors, writers, directors, and teachers. The class began with relaxation, followed by sensory exercises. We spent the rest of the time doing scenes performed by class members and critiqued by Hull and our classmates. Some wrote, directed, and acted in scenes.

I enjoyed this class because I could perform the material I wrote or have others perform my work while observing or directing the scene. It was the first time I heard actors speak the dialogue I had written. It was a benefit that improved my writing enormously. Every few months, we held an evening of performances of pieces that members of the class had written, performed in, or directed. I developed my play, *My Sister My Wife*, in that class. A good friend and classmate, Tara Untiedt, wrote *the Powerpuff Squadron*, a play about women in the Vietnam war that she produced in a Hollywood theatre.

During my time in the class, Dr. Hull was writing her book *Strasberg's Method as Taught by Lorrie Hull*. Surprisingly, no one had ever documented Strasberg's exercises and acting techniques, not even the man himself. Like Syd Field had shared his book with his students, Hull did the same, giving us sections of the book for the various sensory exercises we were working on. In turn, we helped her with our feedback on the writing, how it applied to the exercises, and whether it helped us doing them.

After I was in the class for a while, Lorrie asked if I would like to help with her children's class on Wednesday afternoons. I agreed to do that and got free tuition for Lorrie's class on Tuesday night. It was a great experience working with these pre-teens. They were like sponges. When I gave them improvs, they went into it wholeheartedly. Kids don't have the hang-ups and repressions that we develop as adults. It reminded me of my childhood when we played war or other games, and we fully believed what we were doing.

My other class was on Thursday evening with Marc Marno. He was a tough guy who grew up in Manhattan's Hell's Kitchen. We hit it off from the start. We had similar New York backgrounds, and he wasn't much older than me. He used to call me "*Scungilli*." (That's Italian for conch fish.) I don't know why he called me that. Maybe I looked like a scungilli. Marno had an impressive resume of acting work. I think he burned out in Hollywood, and like many actors, he wasn't getting the types of roles that matched his abilities. So, he quit the business, returned to school, achieved a master's degree, and began teaching at the Institute.

Marc was an excellent teacher who pushed you to always go further into the work. I had many breakthroughs in his class. In one of his earliest critiques of my work, he pointed out, "You have this Woody Allen persona on stage." That surprised me. I liked Woody Allen but wasn't aware I was cloning him in my work. He continued, "It's fun to watch, but it isn't practical for all situations."

I slowly but surely broke that habit. The other thing he helped me do was to return to my street roots and my "New *Yorkese*." I did it through scenes from the *Indian Wants the Bronx*, *American Buffalo*, *The Pope of Greenwich Village*, and other similar types of material. Marno was right about that because I got auditions for tough street guys when I tapped into the New York thing.

The animal exercise was one of my favorites. I worked on it for a long time. It was for developing awareness, observation, and control. Marno suggested working on the ape. Some people studied dogs, cats, and birds. I believe the ape was the most popular among students because of its similarity to humans. I enjoyed going to the L.A. Zoo and watching the apes' behavior for long periods, then coming home and practicing what I observed. For their size, they could move very delicately. They could sit there for a long time, picking insects from their bodies, mates, or children's bodies. Dr. Hull believed Marlon Brando used an elephant in Don Corleone's death scene in *The Godfather* movie. She explained, "It appeared that Brando carried a heavy weight on his shoulders." However, she said, "Brando denied it." But that was how Brando was about his acting.

One of the other fun and exciting things we did in Marno's class was an exercise called "the mask." It wasn't one of the twelve or so sensory exercises. Supposedly, it came from the experimental theatre movement. Marc said, "Putting on a mask could give you permission to do something that you couldn't ordinarily do without the mask."

You created your mask and what you did with it was your choice. People made them out of paper plates or bought masks; others wore paper bags with cutouts for your mouth, nose, and eyes.

I made mine out of a paper bag. I had thought crying was a difficult emotion for me on stage. With my mask on, tears came quickly. It was an eye-opening experience for the performer and to watch classmates reach new heights. This type of exploration was another tool in the actor's repertoire that you could use to achieve a difficult task or an emotional experience.

In Marno's class, I advanced quickly under his tutelage. I progressed through the sensory exercises and my scene work. He was impressed with my progress and admitted me into his advanced class, which consisted of some of the best actors in the school. Amy Madigan, a popular singer, turned actress, and the wife of the actor Ed Harris, had been in the class before I joined it.

In the advanced class, I experimented with music and other ways to get in touch with feelings, places that would influence my behavior in a scene, and objects that would elicit an emotional response or a different result. There were many epiphanies.

Marc Marno, like his mentor, Lee Strasberg, would go off on actors occasionally. He knew when an actor was bullshitting him about what he was working on or wanted to accomplish in the scene. I usually sat somewhere not too far behind Marno in class. I could tell when he was about to blow his top because the veins in his neck seemed to swell under his skin. Sometimes, he would jump on stage to demonstrate something important to the actor and for the benefit of the class. I learned as much from watching other actors as I did when acting.

All the hard work made me cocky enough to audition for the Actors Studio. One of my classmates, a young talented girl, named Margaret O'Keefe, asked me to audition with her in a scene we had been working on in class. Marno disapproved of our audition but helped us to improve the scene. He felt we weren't ready for the Studio. But we went ahead and did it anyway.

The Actors Studio was in West Hollywood, not far from the Strasberg Institute. The theatre space was in a garage behind a big house on the estate of William S. Hart, a movie cowboy, and owned by the City of West Hollywood.

Margaret, my scene partner, was an actress with powerful emotions at her fingertips. Working with her was an amazing experience because she gave you so much to work off of that you were, as they say, "in the moment." I realized that's when real acting happened. When that happens, you are only aware of the other person in the scene. Most actors have a difficult time achieving those heights, not Margaret. Marno used to tell her she had to sit on her emotions more than other actors.

For our Actors Studio audition, we did a scene from the *Shadow Box* by Michael Cristofer. I played Joe, the husband and terminal cancer patient, and Margaret played Maggie, my wife. Our scene went well.

From what I understood, to become a member, you had to show them something they had never seen before—and you had to impress them. Three judges watched the scenes. They were Leonard Nimoy, Ellen Burstyn, and I can't remember who the other one was.

We met back at the Strasberg Institute to celebrate a classmate's birthday following the audition. Larry Parker's Coffee Shop in Beverly Hills offered limousine service to and from the restaurant on your birthday. So, I joined Margaret, two other women, and the birthday girl for the limousine ride and lunch at the restaurant. It took us longer than usual to make the short trip from Hollywood to Beverly Hills because of heavy traffic in a rainstorm. We sat in a large leather semicircle booth at the restaurant with a phone on its back wall. We were there a long time when Margaret picked up the phone and called the Studio to find out how we did. They accepted her into the Studio as an observer. Even though I didn't make it, I was happy for her and felt I would try auditioning again, but I never did.

When I was at the Strasberg Institute, I got to see and hear the man himself. They showed us video-recorded sessions of Strasberg conducting a master class. One summer, he came to the school and invited students to attend a Q&A with him. The famous actress, Shelley Winters, would occasionally teach at the school. She would say to the administrator, "I wanna talk to the kids," in a whiny voice. Sally Kirkland was friends with Robert De Niro and Al Pacino and invited them to talk to us. At the time, neither of them was comfortable nor very good at speaking in public. Nevertheless, the students attending were in awe, and we hung on their every word.

In 1982, I was still studying at the Institute. I was home from work and sick with the flu when I heard that Lee Strasberg died at eighty. I never met the man personally nor had a relationship with him, but I cried over his death. It must have been all that Method training that evoked my emotions—and I didn't need a mask to achieve them.

Lee Strasberg had two wives, Paula, his first passed away, and then he married younger Anna Mizrahi. He had children from both marriages. His second wife, Anna, ran the school and continued to do so after his death. Ellen Burstyn and Al Pacino co-directed the Actors Studio after Strasberg died. Interestingly, the Strasbergs also inherited Marilyn Monroe's estate following her death in 1962.

I continued attending classes at the Institute through 1983 despite teachers at the school claiming that it would take many more years of Method training before you mastered all that was possible. But once again, I was too anxious to get on with my career to put in all that time. It took a while for me to realize how much I had learned. Looking back, it was a positive experience. I felt it was time for me to move on.

I was finding agents to represent me and making inroads with casting directors. After a while, I realized I needed additional skills to get acting work. Eventually, I started to look for a class to improve my cold readings. They called them cold readings, which implied you had never seen the piece before, but you usually got it at least a day before your audition.

FIELDWORK FOR ACTING SCENES

Researching acting scenes that I was working on in my classes was fun. You probably heard how Robert De Nero gained an extraordinary amount of weight to play the part of Jake LaMotta in *Raging Bull*. He also took boxing lessons. Many actors prepare for acting roles by experiencing situations they can apply to a character or scene.

I was one of many actors in my classes that learned to work that way. One of my scene partners, Cathy Sivak, a talented actress, worked on a scene with me from Clifford Odets', *Waiting for Lefty*. We dressed in our oldest, shabbiest clothes, choosing Downtown L.A. for our research. The first exciting thing was at the Pantry Restaurant, an old L.A. landmark. The host sat us at a booth and left us with menus. A waiter dropped off a relish tray, water, and bread and butter. We only glanced at the menu. When the waiter returned to take our order, we asked for two cups of coffee, two bowls of pea soup, bread, and butter. He looked at us with disdain and quickly took the relish tray away. That crushing blow made us realize what it meant to be poor and hungry. When he returned with our order, he placed it on the table and gruffly asked, "Will there be anything else?"

We said, "No."

We slurped our soup, ate our bread, and drank our coffee through the eyes of two poverty-stricken people. We paid our check and left without leaving him a tip. (That was the first and only time I went to the Pantry.)

Then, we wandered around the neighborhood, noting how the homeless lived. Eventually, we walked into a somewhat rundown hotel and sat in the lobby to get warm. That's when we encountered the good in people. A tall, handsome-looking man, probably in his thirties or forties, was behind the desk. He asked, "Can I help you with anything?"

I said, "No, we just wanted to warm up a little. Is that alright?"

"Sit as long as you like."

We must have looked pretty desperate because eventually, he came over to talk to us. He asked, "Where are you from?"

We had prepared our background story before we went out that evening. I answered, "We just got here from Chicago. We're looking for jobs and a place to live."

He eyed us kindly and asked, "What kind of work do you do?"

"I drove a cab in Chicago. But I can do lots of different kinds of work."

He said, "Oh…."

Cathy said, "I've done office work, typing, filing, things like that."

He left and went somewhere in the back. After a while, he returned to the front desk and occasionally looked over at us. Then, he came over again.

Cathy and I thought he would tell us to leave. Instead, he asked, "Where are you staying?"

I said, "In our car."

He looked sympathetically and said, "I can offer you a maintenance position here in the hotel. That's if you are interested." Reacting to the shocked look on our faces, he said, "I can give you a free room in return."

Cathy smiled and said, "Thank you. That's very kind of you."

Looking at her, he said, "I can offer you a front desk job if you're interested."

We were almost speechless. "Thank you for the offer," Cathy said.

I quickly said, "Can we let you know tomorrow?"

"Of course… And stay as long as you like."

We felt uncomfortable about our lies and left shortly after that—what a learning experience it was.

We did the scene in our next class. When we sat down at the front of the stage, Marno asked, "How did you work on the scene?"

We related our research and told him how it helped us prepare for the scene. He asked, what did it give you? We told him how disheartened we felt and got a sense of what it must be like to be homeless and poverty-stricken. "We tried to bring those experiences to the scene."

He commended us on our scene work, and as was usually the case, he made suggestions for bringing more into the scene the next time.

I was working on a scene from Harold Pinter's, *The Dumb Waiter* with a young actor named Michael Wyle. Michael was one of the hot actors in the school that the administration and teachers took a particular interest in. Amy Heckerling, the director of *Fast Times at Ridgemont High*, cast him in that movie. Occasionally, I noticed that there would be a student that the faculty recognized as a unique talent and took an interest in. I would see them whispering about one or another of these exceptionally talented people. They would help them to get work by recommending them to directors, talent agents, managers, and producers that they knew from the Actors Studio or the Strasberg Institute.

I enjoyed working with Michael. He was an unpredictable actor who would make interesting and outlandish choices. I remember him in a play at the Institute in which his pants were wet around his crotch. He kept dabbing at the damp spot on his pants with a napkin.

Michael and I chose to do our research at the old, abandoned house of Harry Houdini in Laurel Canyon. It was across from the movie cowboy, Tom Mix's house. Frank Zappa and his family lived in the Mix house for a few years in the 1960s. It was a hangout for hippies and rock and roll musicians of the sixties and seventies. I lived right up the street from there and passed the Houdini house daily.

We couldn't get into the abandoned house, so we walked around the overgrown, weed-infested property. It was a very dark, scary night. We used those feelings and the bond we established when we performed the scene in class.

On another occasion, I worked with Leslie Bevis, one of the most beautiful women I have ever known. Leslie was tall and thin, with blond hair and sparkling blue eyes. She spoke with a British accent which I presume she picked up while living and modeling in Europe. I believe she was originally from Baltimore. She and Marc Marno were in a relationship. She always sat next to him in the front row of our class and didn't do any acting in class for quite a while. I was pleased when she asked me to work with her. Marno usually suggested what to work on next when we completed a scene to his satisfaction. He said to Leslie, "...You should work on a scene from Noel Coward's *Private Lives*." He turned around, looked at the assembled class, focused on me, and said, "You should work on it with Scungilli." And that's what Leslie and I did.

The scene took place on a terrace on the French Riviera. So, we met at a restaurant called Moonshadows on the beach in Malibu for one of our rehearsals. We improvised the scene while sipping martinis in stemware on the restaurant's balcony, overlooking the crashing waves of the Pacific Ocean. We used sense memory and listened to the waves, felt the dampness in the sea air, and viewed the beauty of the night sky. Despite the alcohol, I remember my hands getting cold from the dampness. We brought those sensory things to the scene when we performed in class. Each time we did *Private Lives* in class was an improvement over the previous one. Leslie went on to have a successful career in movies and TV. I lost track of her after I left the class.

Another actor I enjoyed working with was Scott Ward. He was a very talented young man, and we worked on a scene from *The Pope of Greenwich Village*. For our research, we went to some sleazy Hollywood bars. I took Scott to the Ivar Theatre in

Hollywood, where they had a strip show with completely nude women.

This scene was a big breakthrough for me. Marc Marno pushed me to bring more "street" into my work. I was a guy who grew up on the streets of New York. When I became an actor, I wanted to portray a different me. I unsuccessfully tried to lose my New York accent and make myself more homogenized. In that scene, I played Charlie and let myself have fun being a tough New York street guy. Marno told me how much more commercial that was for me to get work than what I had been doing. And he was right about that.

THE LITTLE OSCAR THEATRE

I had written the one-act play, *My Sister My Wife*, about a brother and sister from an abusive family who lived together as husband and wife. I workshopped it in Lorrie Hull's class and submitted it to several theatres around town. To my surprise, a new theatre in a North Hollywood strip mall named The Little Oscar Theatre liked the play and wanted to do a production.

They had an innovative concept for the theatre. As the theatre's name implies, they awarded little Oscars every evening following the performance of a couple of hours of one-act plays. Audience members received a ballot upon entering the theatre. I believe the entries were the best performance by an actor and the best performance by an actress. There may have been other categories like Best Play and Best Director.

Set in the 1970s, my play had two characters, a male and a female in their twenties. As the play unfolded, the audience discovered that this brother and sister had an abusive father, and their mother recently passed away from cancer. Drugs and sex helped them deal with the pain and reality of their lives.

The director cast a young black male and a young black female, both exceptional actors. I was disappointed on opening night because Anita couldn't be there; she had classes that night that she couldn't miss.

I was impressed with my actors' performances, thrilled to see something I created on stage and hear the words I wrote performed. I eagerly attended every show, and every night my actors won the most votes and the nightly best-acting awards. And Anita got to see the show before it closed.

That's when I realized the power of theatre and how it seemed a lot easier to get a play mounted than to write spec screenplays. I knew then that there were many more plays in my future, but that was the only one produced in Hollywood.

WORKING ON THE SOAPS

I never saw myself as a soap opera-type and never watched them. I knew they always had beautiful women and the men were usually hunks; I was neither. However, I submitted my pictures and resumes anyway. The soaps provided a good training ground for actors and an opportunity to work on an AFTRA (American Federation of Television and Radio Actors) show, fulfilling the requirements to qualify for the Screen Actors Guild membership. So, I was surprised when I got a call from the casting office of *General Hospital*. The casting director at the time was Marvin Paige. I didn't even have to audition. They gave me a call time to get to the set the next day.

I played a drunk in a bar scene with an unshaven gritty look. It was a pivotal moment in the plot. Someone paid off the waitress to keep her mouth shut about something. I got up as a drunk and staggered out of the bar. But on my way out, I bumped into the waitress and accidentally grabbed hold of the pocket on her apron, it ripped, and cash fell all over the floor. This was supposed to be the big Friday show surprise. The other actors in the scene were two of the show's male stars. I presume the waitress may have had a recurring role. I was what they called a day player, just there for that scene, but day players might also appear in one or more scenes.

Several years later, I had an opportunity to work on the soap opera *Days of Our Lives*. Once again, I didn't have to audition; they just gave me the part. I played a Salvation Army bell ringer dressed in the uniform with a tripod and hanging bucket at my side. I had a few lines in a scene with Lisa Rinna, one of the show's attractive stars. When she deposited some money in my bucket, I was so nervous about getting my lines out that I kept stepping on hers. I guess they expected that to happen. Lisa was lovely and never complained. The director was also patient, sitting in a control room off the set. He didn't address me, only Lisa. I felt uncomfortable, but I settled down and nailed it after several takes.

Working on the soaps was interesting. Everyone works very hard, whether on the production crew or on-camera talent. There was a run-through in the morning, and then following lunch, they shot the show from beginning to end. There were several sets on the sound stage. They alerted you in your dressing room to come up when it got close to shooting your scene. They moved the actors into the set, and the cameras followed. They would shoot each scene and efficiently go from one to the next. Mine took place outdoors.

I learned that sometimes technical problems cause them to go back and re-shoot the entire show. They didn't have any issues the day I worked, and they released us.

Those were the only two soaps I ever worked on. I wished there were more, and I tried getting on them by regularly submitting my picture and resume, but it never happened.

A SPOOKY HOLLYWOOD TALE

This tale begins in Africa. My friend Marilyn went to the African continent on vacation. While there, she fell in love with an African man, and they married. Besides falling in love with her new husband, she also acquired a fondness for the area's art and opened a gallery in West Hollywood on chic Melrose Avenue.

We attended the opening. Marilyn introduced us to Mustafa, the African gentleman who managed her gallery. We admired several pieces. Anita wanted to buy something, and we looked at a mask. Mustafa explained, "This mask was probably worn when the tribe's king came to visit. You are not allowed to look at or talk to the king without a mask." He went on to point out its features to us. It had seashells, beads, and other small objects embedded into it. He said, "Those features indicate to the king your wealth and status in the community. A prominent member of a village wore this mask."

We decided to buy it. I don't remember how much we paid. They wrapped it up, and we took it home. When we got home, we just left the mask wrapped until the following evening, then found a place for it on one of our living room walls.

The next day, we had a new cleaning lady clean our house. She was still there when I came home from work, and she was beside herself. I asked what had happened. She was practically in tears and blurted out, "I was cleaning the shutters, and they just fell apart." It was true. The little slats just fell off one of our shutters. I told her it was alright and not to worry about it. We were able to repair it quickly.

A day or two later, I got a call about a movie I had auditioned for. The person on the phone told me they wanted me for a different role than I had read. A friend familiar with the production said, "Oh, that's the part where you are in bed with a real porno star."

I'm not a prude or opposed to pornographic movies, but there was something seedy about the project. So, I turned down the part and didn't think anything else about it. There may have been some other unusual things that happened that week, but we didn't pay much attention to them.

But Sunday night was the topper. It was about ten o'clock; we heard screeching brakes outside on the street, then a crashing car tearing up the steps of our neighbor's house, taking out all of their wrought-iron railings and ours. Its forward motion stopped when it hit the corner of our house; the house shook from the impact.

I looked out the window, and there was a black Mercedes sedan upside down in the street. I opened the window and saw a young man crawling out the driver's window. I asked him, "Are you alright?"

When he answered, he sounded dizzy or drunk. "I'm... okay."

He skidded on the wet street—wet from someone's sprinklers up the road—lost control and hit our houses. He mentioned something about a fight with his boyfriend. He had to call the boyfriend to pick him up. Miraculously, he survived without a scratch.

I don't know how we concluded that the mask had something to do with these unpredictable incidents. So, I called Marilyn on Monday morning and told her what had happened since we brought the mask home. She immediately said, "Bring it back!" We brought it back that evening. Mustafa didn't question us; he accepted that the incidents were associated with the mask. He told us, "Sometimes these objects are stolen from their tribal homes and owners. This mask must have bad *jujus*."

He told us he could exchange it for something else in the store. We found a mahogany giraffe. The craziness stopped as soon as we got rid of that mask. It's funny because the cleaning lady knocked that giraffe over many times while dusting our furniture. Whenever she did, the ears usually broke, and she glued them back.

WRITING GROUPS

The first writing group I belonged to was during a writer's strike in the late eighties. My friend Ray Forman lived up the street from me. There was a writers' strike going on in Hollywood. We decided it might be a good opportunity to write and sell a screenplay. It was funny how we both bought houses on the same street in Laurel Canyon, unbeknownst to each other at the time.

I met Ray through our wives, who worked at CBS at the time. Ray and Betty were also from Long Island, New York, and we had a lot in common. Ray's father, Bill Forman, was a musician who transitioned to opening a music copyist company. Music copyists proofread musical scores and prepare individual parts for each instrument in the band. Ray worked for his dad. They provided services for the Carol Burnett TV show in New York and followed her to Los Angeles when she moved the show to CBS Television City in Hollywood.

It was common to hear about staged car accidents on the streets and freeways of L.A. I suggested to Ray, "Let's write about a gang who stages accidents to collect insurance claims. And an evil judge heads up the gang." In our screenplay, the bad guys developed a large truck that would cause massive, staged accidents. A tow truck-driving older woman, a tough and crusty type, and her son, a freeway-loving car enthusiast, were the only ones trying to foil the plot.

A friend of Ray's invited us to join a writing group in Venice, California, that he belonged to. The guy who ran it lived close to the beach. It was an eclectic group. One of the members was an aerospace engineer. He had an analytical mind and was trying to find a formula for writing screenplays. The man who organized and ran the group had a script about a married couple stalked on the Pacific Coast Highway. Another writer in the group was developing a screenplay based on Arthur Conan Doyle's hundred-year-old parrot, who had a library of crime dramas that he could recall from living with Doyle.

Our *Freeway Freaks* screenplay was much longer than the preferred one-hundred twenty-page format. We never completed it. It had every sight gag and joke we could think of. We never polished it to the point where we could approach anyone to produce it. The group eventually broke up, as writing groups tend to do.

Several years later, my friend Tara Untiedt started a writing group. She called it The Midnight Writers. Most of the members had been in a high-concept pitching class together. This group jelled and went on for several years. It wasn't until some members moved out of L.A. that the group finally broke up. While I was in it, I wrote my screenplay; *Someday You'll Be Old,* inspired by Anita's mom. My character Mildred Myers leads a tenement revolt against the City of New York when they try to raze her home of over thirty years for a condo development. There was some initial interest in a possible sitcom. Eventually, I adapted and expanded this story into my novel *Unassisted Living*. Many excellent screenplays came out of the group. Some of the writers sold their scripts. Others went on to produce movies and write books.

Writing groups are an excellent sounding board for ideas and a place to get feedback, especially when you are a new writer. They provided the kick in the ass that most of us needed to pursue our writing ambitions. When you know that a meeting is coming up, it makes you sit down and write. With good writers in a group, it can be most beneficial.

In the next chapter, Anita talks about her student film.

ANITA'S SHORT FILM—SATIN DOLLS

In 1983, in my senior year at Columbia College, I had the opportunity to produce and direct a documentary or a fictional short about twenty to thirty minutes in length. I wasn't sure what to do. Bob suggested, "Why don't you make a movie about your rock and roll band?"

In the sixties and seventies, my sister and I had a band, the Satin Dolls. Our theme song was Count Basie's *Satin Doll* played to a rock and roll beat. Bob offered to write the screenplay with my help. We liked what we wrote, and I submitted it for approval. My instructor gave me the go-ahead. That set the wheels in motion. It would become one of our favorite projects and our first film project together. Bob wrote a part for himself, the character of Frankie, a Brooklyn garbage man and the girls' so-called manager. In this fictional account, the band practiced for their first paying gig. Their stubborn Italian American father forbid them from playing in a nightclub, and to make matters worse, he locked up their instruments. It tore their family apart, pitting mom and dad against each other.

Besides being in the film as an actor, Bob helped with the production. He was excited to be on the production side of things for a change, and an excellent learning experience. The first thing we realized was that many things go into making a film. We had to cast it, find locations, record music, acquire supplies and props, put a crew together, make costumes, and get equipment, all on a minimal budget. We also put some of our own money into the project. The school provided lights, light stands, sound equipment, cameras, and some film.

Our biggest challenge was making Los Angeles look like Brooklyn. Thanks to our friend, Ann Hyatt, we found a way to solve that. Ann was going to New York for a few days. I asked her, "Can you go to Brooklyn and shoot photos of houses, buildings, and street signs?" We used the photos at the film's beginning to establish that the setting was Brooklyn. Ann also had a small acting role in the movie.

We needed three young women in their twenties or early thirties for the band. We advertised casting notices in *DramaLogue*. We had several other male and female roles as well. There was an overwhelming response. Casting is always a challenge, especially for student films. You want good actors, but there is no pay. Actors do student films for the experience, the chance to work with budding filmmakers, and ultimately obtain film on themselves to showcase their talent.

We also had to cast a father and mother in their forties or fifties. We were lucky when Lew Dauber came to our house to audition. He wasn't a typical Brooklyn guy and was much younger than we imagined. I felt he could play the part with makeup and a little grey on the sides of his thinning hair. He captured the essence of my father and had the right attitude.

We realized that Lew was correct when he complained that he was too angry in most of his scenes. So, Bob wrote a scene where he and his daughter shared a sweet, intimate moment. It helped soften him a little. Following the movie, Lew would become a life-long friend.

Lew was in a local stage production of *Bleacher Bums,* and he suggested a woman in the play for the girls' mother. That worked out well too. Helen Siff got the part. She was also much younger than we imagined for the mom but had the right attitude to play a Brooklyn mother/homemaker. These two roles were probably the hardest to cast.

There was also a part for a raunchy standup comedian. I found a funny actor named John Jackson for the part. One of our more pleasant surprises was Johnn-Benn, our hairdresser for the shoot. In exchange for helping with hair, he asked for an acting role in the movie. He was thrilled to play a bartender in the nightclub. He fell in love with acting and went on to have a career in film, TV, commercials, and the stage. Benn claimed *Satin Dolls* was his big break and was grateful for the part.

As for the girls in the band, we received many submissions. We cast Mags Kavanaugh as my sister, the band's leader. Lori Zogab, an outstanding young actress, got to play me, the band's drummer. We got lucky with Lisa Marie Gurley, a fine actress and a fabulous singer. Bob and I bonded with the girls, and our friendship continued after the film.

Members of the crew were classmates. Our friend and fellow student Eric Grufman had the critical cinematographer position, responsible for lighting the production. A Swiss exchange student and friend, Jurg Ebe, was our cameraman. He already had a string of professional productions in Switzerland under his belt. Other students from Columbia College came and pitched in as needed.

Locations are always a pesky problem for professional filmmakers as well as students. In the Southern California area, people are aware that studio productions pay homeowners well for the use of their property. Film students don't usually have the funds to pay for locations. They depend on people's generosity and patience. Another problem that arises when using someone's property—production companies have a terrible reputation for trashing places they use and disrespecting the owners. We needed several locations: a house, a basement, a park-like setting, and a nightclub.

We don't remember how we got to use a house in Torrance for the girls' home. Someone who knew someone referred us to a sweet older woman who let us use her house. I remember Bob, Eric, and I met with her. Eric looked over the place for lighting considerations. The woman agreed to let us use her home for two days. The four of us sat around her dining room table, held hands, and she said a prayer for the success of the movie.

The basement of the fictional house where the band practiced was in Jurg Ebe's friend's house in Glendale. We spent one day shooting there. Then had another day on the grounds of U.C.L.A., where we shot a scene of the girls during their work lunch hour in a park-like setting. We also had a New York-style hot dog cart that someone lent us for that day.

The nightclub was more challenging to acquire. It was supposed to be the raunchy, infamous Crazy Country Club in Bay Ridge, Brooklyn, where the original Satin Dolls played their first professional gig.

Bob and I were walking along the Sunset Strip near the Whiskey A-Go-Go and the Roxy, looking for a place to shoot the nightclub scenes. We noticed an open door. Inside, it looked like a small bar or a nightclub. When we went inside, several young guys were sitting around talking. I said, "We need a club to shoot a student film for two days."

To our surprise, they said, "You can do it here, but you have to do it very soon because the Department of Water and Power is about to turn off the electricity." They laughed and said, "We haven't paid the bill in a long time."

"We want to do it this weekend. If that's okay," I said,

"Great. We use this place as a private club to hang out in, but we also like to use it for artistic purposes—like your film."

We were excited to have the location, and we all shook hands. That Saturday and Sunday, we shot there. I had to fill it with extras for the movie's final scenes. Our cinematographer, Eric, wanted to light the girls' performance in red light and then hit Gurley, the lead singer, with a spotlight. The excess drain on the electrical system burned out some circuit breakers. We didn't know about the burned-out breakers at the time.

Eric wasn't happy because he couldn't get the lighting he wanted for the scene.

Weeks before the production, I had to get musicians to record the music and vocals. There was a music school in Hollywood, and several student musicians volunteered to play and record the music. Lisa Gurley and the two girls sang *Satin Doll*, *Mustang Sally*, and *Break It to Me Gently*. So, the music played at the club, and Gurley, Kavanaugh, and Zogab lip-synced to the recorded music while they faked playing instruments. It was a challenge in a student film to have recorded music to lip-sync, but we pulled it off.

We spent Saturday at the club shooting a scene with Frankie on the phone talking to Toni (Mags Kavanaugh) about how he was trying to find instruments for the girls. Then we set up for the shoot the following day. The crew set lights and the band's instruments in the front of the room. The guys who lent us the place hung out there late into the night. Bob and I slept there in the red booths because we were concerned about our musical instruments and film equipment.

Except for the lighting problem, the shoot went smoothly. The film ended with Lisa Marie Gurley singing Brenda Lee's, *Break It to Me Gently*, which made the tiny hairs on your neck stand up.

Recently, Eric Grufman related a moment to us that he has always been fond of. He said, "While shooting the club scene, Lisa sang, *Break It to Me Gently* in an extended take, and we ran out of film in the magazine long before we could get everything we wanted. I quietly and privately told Anita she should cut, but Anita and everyone on the crew was enjoying Gurley's performance so much that Anita said to pretend to continue shooting so Gurley and all the crew could experience the sheer joy of the moment. And we did. How sweet of Anita!"

I spent my last few months at Columbia College editing the film, adding sound effects, polishing it, and cutting the negative. When I finished postproduction, I had a screening at the school and received rave reviews from faculty and students. We had another guest screening at a venue in Santa Monica called The House. Everyone enjoyed what we created. Following that, we entered *Satin Dolls* in several film festivals.

I earned a Bachelor of Arts in Film Production when graduation rolled around. On top of that, I was Valedictorian and spoke at the graduation ceremony in one of the ballrooms at the Universal Sheraton Hotel. My mom came from Florida for the event and was proud of my accomplishments. Bob was proud of me too. I was sad my father, Cosmo, never got to see me graduate. He had passed away a few years earlier due to asbestos cancer.

Bob gave me a little grey cockatiel for a graduation present, which we named Sushi because we had recently started to eat sushi. We gave the bird that name because we didn't know whether it was male or female. It turned out that Sushi was a boy.

Many of the people who helped us with *Satin Dolls* went on to successful film careers. Shortly after we finished the film, Lisa Gurley and Bob worked together on a beer commercial and an experimental film Lisa's friend directed. They shot it in the storm drains in Studio City off and on for several months. Lew Dauber, Helen Siff, and John Jackson all went on to have successful film careers. Jurg Ebe returned to

Switzerland, where he wrote, produced, and directed several feature films.

We enjoyed making this film, and many cast and crew remained friends. We are thankful to everyone that helped. After that, I wanted to be a film director and producer. I felt I had a good eye and a comfortable rapport with actors. Those four years at Columbia College helped me focus on my goals in the entertainment industry.

Bob will tell you about the hijacking/hostage play in the next chapter.

GATE 11 & HOSTAGES IN THE PARK

Gate 11 opened at the Burbank Theatre Guild in 1985. This small theatre was in a one-story building in a Burbank park. The park had baseball fields, swings, and lovely places to sit and relax. This was the play's world premiere. It was described as a hostage/hijacker drama by J. Reed. The author could have been anonymous because we never met J. Reed. There were twenty-plus characters in the play. For the show, the theatre looked like the inside of a passenger plane. Upon entering, the audience was unaware they would participate as hostages in an airplane hijacking.

The theatre was under the artistic direction of two young actors. This was their first production. The play's executive producer was Joan E. Nelson, a woman from Las Vegas. We found out later in the run that the playwright J. Reed was Joan Nelson. Her six-year-old son was in the play, and she wrote it as a vehicle to help promote his acting career. Gate 11 refers to an airline arrival/departure gate.

At the time, airline hijackings were a common occurrence. The author was making a statement about them. I played President Assad, a character inspired by Muammar Gaddafi, or Saddam Hussein of Iraq. I was directly responsible for the hijacking. I loved playing the role of a dictator.

In the first act, armed hijackers sitting among the audience members take over the plane. At intermission, the hijackers led the audience out of the theatre into the park and, with guns, surrounded the hostages. Opening weekend, several kids riding bikes through the park noticed what was going on and reported it to their parents, who subsequently called the police. The entire audience and actors were back in the theatre, and Act 2 was underway when we heard a helicopter circling overhead. We were unaware that the police had arrived, and the cast didn't find out until after the show.

The incident caused quite a stir and was even on the local TV news. It boosted our attendance for the rest of the run, and we had sold-out shows. Some people believed that Joan Nelson called the cops for the publicity and the story about the kids was untrue.

One evening after the show, the late actor Roscoe Lee Browne came backstage to congratulate us on a great performance. I will never forget Browne saying, "You guys scared the shit out of me," in his gravelly voice. A friend told me, "When we used to hike Mt. Cahuenga, we would pass by a quaint little cottage on the way to the trailhead, and one day out stepped Roscoe Lee Browne. It was his house. He invited us in for a drink, and we spent a delightful few hours with him. What a nice man."

The play was an excellent opportunity for me as an actor. There were so many good actors in it you couldn't help but shine. I dressed as an Arab with a turban (which was a little controversial for a Middle East despot to wear a turban, but that's what the director wanted.) I also wore robes and spoke with an accent. We received favorable reviews. An agent who came to the play liked me and signed me as a client.

Ironically, a few years later, that agent and her agency ran into financial trouble, and Joan Nelson took over the business in which I was still a client. Joan liked me and, for a short time, represented me. After that, I don't know what happened to the Nelsons; they may have gone back to Las Vegas. I had already moved on and had a new theatrical agent.

JOINING THE UNIONS

If you want to be a professional actor in Hollywood, you must be in a union. There were the American Federation of Television and Radio Actors (AFTRA) and the Screen Actors Guild (SAG) during my time. Most TV work required you to be in AFTRA, and film work fell under the jurisdiction of SAG. (The Screen Actors Guild was the more prestigious of the two.) For years, the goal was to merge the two unions—many actors were members of both; eventually, they merged, naming the new union SAG-AFTRA.

There were also non-union productions. They were an excellent place to start your career and get some on-screen experience which you could also use on your sample reel. When doing non-union work, it didn't take long to figure out why the unions were there to protect you from unscrupulous producers who took advantage of actors. At the time, the Screen Actors Guild had about eighty-thousand actors, of which ninety-eight percent were out of work.

Despite the high unemployment—getting into SAG was difficult. AFTRA was the easiest to join. You could just pay the initiation fee (mine was $250). That entitled you to work television contracts. It also provided a means to join SAG. Here's how that worked. I was on a soap and then *Archie Bunker's Place* a couple of times. They were atmosphere or background jobs, also referred to as extras. These were excellent learning experiences, and they paid well. Carroll O'Connor, who played Archie Bunker, wanted to give young actors a break and hired them for his new show, which came along after *All in the Family*. I got the job because I sent the casting director Jane Murray my picture and resume.

I had already worked on the soap opera *General Hospital,* so I took my pay stubs for the three times I worked on those AFTRA shows and applied for admission to the Screen Actors Guild. I don't remember the membership lady's name, but when I went to see her, she said, "I need to see your contracts for the work."

"I don't have any contracts, only my pay stubs," I pleaded. After a few more minutes of banter, she accepted my membership request. All of this took place in the guild's lobby on Sunset Boulevard. One of the other ways to qualify for membership was to have secured a SAG role in a movie. You could also get in by having a letter from a producer saying they had hired you for a film, confirming your potential employment.

The work requirement through AFTRA was an acceptable method for many actors. A friend suggested a hair-brained scheme to go on Chuck Barris's TV *Gong Show* and do a funny scene. That could qualify you to join the union. But we never did that.

Shortly after applying to SAG, they invited me to an orientation where I paid my initiation fee (which I believe was also $250). That day we were shooting

Satin Dolls at the Torrance house. I had to leave the shoot for my orientation.

While waiting for the orientation to begin, I recalled an experience I had a few years before. There was a young guy in my acting class. I gave him information about some background casting agencies that got me extra work. The next time I saw the kid, he said, "Hey, thanks for that information. They called me to work on a production. When I got to the set, I introduced myself to the director. I told him that I was there for the day, and if he needed me for anything, come and get me. A little while later, one of the assistant directors told me they were going to give me a few lines in a scene." The result of which got him into SAG. I wished I had that kind of *chutzpah*.

The SAG member facilitating the orientation was Daryl Anderson, who played Animal, the photographer on the *Lou Grant Show*. I was excited to get into the union. The meeting was held in the big boardroom. Anderson discussed the benefits of being in SAG. One significant benefit was SAG health insurance. In all my years as a member, I never worked enough to qualify for health insurance. The other thing about the meeting was union rule #1—never work non-union. That stuck with me, and no matter how desperate I was for work, I never worked non-union after that.

It took an effort to get my membership, and I was proud when I got my SAG card. It opened doors to better agents, auditions, and SAG jobs. That was an exhilarating day for me.

Following the orientation, I had to go to the post-production house to screen the dailies we had shot the day before for *Satin Dolls*. Still high from my orientation, I sat in a small screening room in a comfy chair like a big-time producer. I talked to the projectionist in the booth through the telephone at my fingertips and viewed the dailies. I didn't know what I was looking for; however, I didn't see anything wrong with the dailies. They looked good to me.

MY FAVORITE CASTING DIRECTOR

I met casting director Sally Powers at a workshop. They were so-called workshops where you pay for the privilege of doing a scene with a partner, a monologue, or a cold reading for a guest casting director, director, producer, manager, or agent. Sometimes they were assistants for a casting director and got paid for being there. A number of these popped up all over town. The actors' unions frowned upon them and even tried to abolish them. But it was an opportunity to meet and show these people what you could do. I tried to take advantage of the opportunity.

Sally Powers was a long-time casting director and was well respected in the business. I went to her workshop because, at the time, she was casting director for the popular TV series *Hill Street Blues.* I don't believe Sally did it for the money. She was earnestly looking for new talent and faces. I liked her from the start, and she seemed interested in me.

Around the holidays, I usually put something together to send those in the industry with whom I had a relationship or wanted to meet. I put together a little Italian cookbook with some favorite appetizers, entrees, and desserts. I also included my headshot and resume. I never received a thank you or any response. Sally

Powers was the only one who sent me a little note of thanks. I was so impressed.

My goal was to work on *Hill Street Blues,* so I was excited when my agent, Doris Ross, called to say I had an audition for the show. I was working full-time as a technical writer in a job I hated. I told my employers that I was an actor when they hired me, and they didn't mind my taking time off to audition and do acting work. I always made up any hours I missed. My audition was for the part of a thief who got a tattoo every time he held up a drug store. The audition went well because Doris called me at work a couple of days later, laughing, and said, "They want to know if you have a hairy back." We both thought it was humorous. They wanted to know because they were going to tattoo me. I got the part thanks to my hairless back.

The make-up person was Bob Westmoreland from the famous Hollywood make-up artist family. At first, he used tattoo stencils, but he didn't like how they came out, so he drew several tattoos on my back and arms.

We filmed at a location in downtown Los Angeles. Grace Zabriskie (*Twin Peaks* TV series), a character actress, was the tattoo artist. The other actors in the scene were the series regulars Kile Martin (playing J.D. La Rue), Taurean Blacque (playing Neal Washington), and Peter Jurasik (playing Sid the Snitch). The episode was called *Das Blues,* and Scott Brazil, one of the producers, directed.

The actors in the scene with me were wonderful to work with and helpful to a newbie like me. Unfortunately, they cut my lines in the final on-air product. My mother said, "We saw your ear, but you didn't say nothin'." It's not unusual to wind up on the editor's cutting room floor.

After that, Sally kept calling me for different shows she was casting, one of which was *Matlock* starring Andy Griffith. At the time, I didn't' know that he and I shared the same birthday, June 1st. I might have been able to have a conversation with him. He merely greeted me, and we went on with the scene. I played a hotdog vendor with the umbrella and stand. I handed him a hot dog, and he offered me tickets to Gilbert and Sullivan. I smiled and said, "Where they fightin'?" He responded, "It's a musical."

We were filming outside near USC. In the afternoon, someone in an apartment building across the street turned up the volume on their TV, playing the *Mayberry* theme song. Andy laughed and said, "That's why I didn't work for ten years after that show." People remembered him as Andy, the sheriff of Mayberry, something that happens to many stars who are typecast because of a character they played.

I wanted to be on the new Steve Bochco cop show, *NYPD*. Sally came through with several auditions. I read for Bochco and the producers a few times. While waiting for my turn to audition once, one of the creators/writers, David Milch, who created *Deadwood*, stopped to talk. I was sitting next to a guy who was a boxer. Milch struck up a conversation with the fighter and me. He said, "We were looking for a boxer like you and couldn't find anyone." I never landed a part on the show.

Sally Powers provided the key to opening doors for me. *Hill Street* was my first SAG job. I am forever grateful for her confidence in me.

In the next chapter, Anita talks about her career in film production.

Our friend writer, actress, director, and producer, Tara Untiedt.

Mary Cannarili, Anita's Mom.

Anita took this headshot.

Our friend, Lew Dauber, played the girl's father in *Satin Dolls*.

Lori Zogaib the drummer in the *Satin Dolls* movie.

YOU'RE INVITED
TO THE SCREENING
OF

 An Anita Puglisi Film

Date: July 11, 1984 - Wednesday
Time: 7:30pm–Reception
9:00pm–Screening
Place: THE HOUSE
1329B 5th Street
Santa Monica, CA

Please RSVP if attending (by 7/9)

Invitation to our *Satin Dolls* screening.

Our birds, Sushi, on the left, and Nattie on the right.

In our house on Wonderland Avenue in L.A.

Our ski cabin in Mammoth one winter.

Anita's 1978 Mercedes 450SL.

Daughter Deb Sanquiche with Alex and DJ.

Grandsons Alex and DJ at Disney's character breakfast.

Anita's office window to nowhere.

Moving Day 1998.

The front of our Mt. Crested Butte house.

Back of our Mt. Crested Butte house.

BON VOYAGE!

Taken at Gunnison Airport after vacationing with Steve and Jennifer Evans. Bob and Anita got food poisoning. Jennifer made wonton soup to settle their stomachs. Steve had to work throughout this vacation, so he chartered the plane to get back to Durango and fly home from there. Bob stayed in Crested Butte a few more days. Anita flew back to L.A. and then went to Japan for business.

ANITA'S CAREER MOVES

Even before I received my degree from Columbia College, I had befriended several women in the film industry and cultivated a network of a few influential women. At the same time, my position at Ed Hansen and Associates became uncertain. The company had fallen on hard times with fewer and fewer projects in the pipeline.

One of my classmates, Mandy Marsh, a young, attractive blonde, told me about a negative cutting job at Wexler & Company where she worked. I took the position working freelance. I had to cut the final negatives for all types of film projects. I had experience cutting the negative for *Satin Dolls* and other film projects I had worked on at school, but the job scared me. Cutting your negative was one thing but doing it for other people's films could be nerve-wracking. But I became more confident as time went on. Cutting a film's negative was one of the last steps to preparing the film's final print for processing.

After a while, I moved on to work at the Playboy Channel. My friends Pam Scrape and Ann Hyatt both worked there. Ann was production manager on several of the channel's shows. They hired me as a freelance production assistant. My boss, Don Kline, was the producer of the shows. Don was well over six feet tall, prematurely bald, and had a pleasing, friendly way. Don and his wife, Penny, became good friends. Penny was petite and only about five feet tall. They made an interesting-looking couple. We went on ski trips together and to parties and social events. We enjoyed several New Year's Eves at the Kline's. Don, a native of Buffalo, New York, introduced us to one of that city's favorite foods—beef on weck. The beef was roast beef, and weck was a butter-coated roll with salt and caraway seeds sprinkled over the top and baked. He sliced the roast beef thin, dipped it in au jus, placed it on the roll, and served it with more au jus and horseradish on the side.

I enjoyed working at Playboy. Their offices were in the Playboy building on Sunset Boulevard, one of the former Playboy Clubs. It was the closest I ever lived to work, only minutes from our Laurel Canyon home. Working there, I met lots of interesting and talented people. We shot some shows at the Playboy Mansion with beautiful naked Playmates scattered around the lush grounds. Once, we were shooting at the mansion's grotto, and a few naked women swam up and were curious about what was happening. The male members of the production crew enjoyed that.

When they offered Ann Hyatt a Production Manager position at the Disney Studios in the newly formed Home Video Department, she traded her rabbit ears for mouse ears and left Playboy. To replace her, they hired Barbara Bracher. Barbara was a young, attractive, blonde dynamo. Barbara and I got along great and worked well together. We were both ambitious and hardworking. On one of our projects, we worked all night. Bob was surprised the following morning when Barbara and I showed up at our house to freshen up and go back to work. We worked around the clock to finish our project in time to air on the Playboy Channel.

I worked at Playboy for about a year until I had to have unexpected surgery. While I was recovering, most of the shows I worked on were canceled. Eventually, I returned to work on the few remaining shows on the channel. But it wasn't long before they canceled those too. Don Kline was also moving on.

Shortly after the September 11th terrorist attacks, we found out that the wife of President George Bush's Solicitor General, Ted Olson, was on Flight 77 that crashed into the Pentagon. She was the former Barbara Bracher. After working at Playboy, she went to law school and became a federal prosecutor and TV commentator. She divorced her first husband and married Olson.

Bob talks about surprise phone calls in Hollywood in the next chapter.

WHEN YOUR PHONE RINGS IN HOLLYWOOD

If you are a Hollywood actor, you are most likely waiting for your phone to ring. It could be your agent, a manager, a producer, a director, or a casting director. They could be calling to offer you an audition or, even better, an acting role and a paying job. They say your phone can ring and change your life forever. As an actor, I never felt I had one of those life-changing experiences, just small ones but very exciting.

One of my favorite stories was when I was walking down Burbank Boulevard in Burbank, and my pager sounded off. I looked at the displayed number and didn't recognize it. From the area code, I knew it was a local call. There was a phone booth nearby. It was before I owned a cell phone.

I called the number on my pager, and Scott, the casting director for *The Tonight Show with Jay Leno,* answered. It surprised me. He was very professional and courteous. He wanted to know if I could come to work with them the next day. My mind screamed with excitement. I wanted to say, *ARE YOU KIDDING!* No audition was necessary. Jay was taking the show to Las Vegas the following week, and they wanted me for a poker scene that would air on one of the Vegas shows.

I don't know for sure how I got the call. I always wanted to be on the Johnny Carson show, so I submitted my picture and resume every few months. I never heard from them, but my submissions must have remained in their files when Leno took over. At least they didn't wind up in the trash. That was another time my perseverance paid off.

That first gig on *The Tonight Show* was a comedy skit with me at a poker table in the fictitious Johnny Stunad's Hotel and Casino. Jay was in the scene narrating the action. They asked if I wanted to draw any cards—I pleaded the Fifth Amendment.

That was the beginning of my relationship with Jay Leno and his show. They would call me from time to time and have me come into work, or I would call them. For the first time in my acting career, I could pick up the phone, call a casting person, get them on the phone, and ask if they had any work for me. They were always fun comedy skits, usually shot before or after that evening's show.

For that first show, I shared a dressing room with another gentleman. I don't know if he was a guest that night or what. After that, a blue card with my name was on my dressing room door whenever I went back to work there, and I had a dressing room to myself.

On one occasion, I met a guy named Jack Coen. We were in an acting class and did a scene together. I knew he did stand-up but didn't know he became one of the writers on the show. On another occasion, Harry Connick Jr. was a guest. I had just seen him in the movie *Hope Floats*. It was his first starring role. I told him how much I enjoyed it. He was so humble and thanked me. We had a friendly conversation while they applied our makeup.

Jay would have his version of Hollywood's holiday parade every holiday season. Jay's parade floats usually featured a reenactment of some current news item. One year, I played a drunk on an airline flight. In the actual case, when they cut off the alcohol for the passenger, he climbed onto the drink trolley, dropped his pants, and took a crap on the cart. (I didn't re-create the drunk's actions. I just had my pants tastefully down as I sat on the trolley.) Another year, I played a tax preparer punching out his partner in their bankrupted, Jacoby and Meyers, income tax preparation firm.

At the time, and because of the lousy economy, adult children were moving back home to live in their parent's basement. I played the father of one of those kids, beating my son with the newspaper want ads to go out and look for a job.

It was always fun to hang out in the show's green room, where there was usually pizza, one of Leno's favorite foods. Leno would be there sometimes to chat with. Walking onto any studio lot in Hollywood was always an honor and a thrill. You never knew who you were going to see.

In the next chapter, Anita tells what happened when her phone rang in Hollywood.

WHEN ANITA'S PHONE RANG IN HOLLYWOOD

I received a couple of life-changing phone calls. After Playboy, I started doing temporary secretarial work. I was also doing freelance production work for Disney.

One day, while on a business call with an associate at Disney, an operator interrupted the call. I ended the Disney call and took the incoming one. It was someone from a temp agency I had been working for. They wanted to know if I was available to work at the actor Jimmy Stewart's business manager's office to work for Mr. Stewart. It was where he also kept an office for himself. An hour later, I was sitting in front of the long-legged legend taking dictation. They were letters to fans that wrote to him. It was thrilling. I was with the famous actor listening to his slow drawl. Jimmy and the business manager liked me. After a few weeks, they offered me a permanent position as Mr. Stewart's secretary. I had nothing else going for me at the time, so I accepted the job. And Jimmy Stewart was as nice as his on-screen persona.

Bob was impressed when he came to the office and met Mr. Stewart. Bob said to Jimmy, "It's nice meeting you."

And Jimmy said, "It's nice meeting *you*," emphasizing the "you."

Mr. Stewart was unassuming. He drove an old Volvo, and his wife Gloria drove their Rolls Royce. He wore an old beat-up fishing hat that his good friend Henry Fonda gave him. The rest of his dress was casual. When he went on trips, he would ask me to get him twenty-five dollars. He didn't have to spend much when he traveled for appearances. They provided him with everything he needed. On the other hand, Gloria Stewart, his wife, would call when they were going away and ask me to get her a lot more money.

We always enjoyed Mr. Stewart on *the Tonight Show* with Johnny Carson even before I worked for him. During my tenure as his secretary, we would see him on the Carson show, and I would say, "Look how he hopped on stage." I couldn't believe he was the same eighty-year-old I was in the office with earlier that day.

At Christmas time, there was always a small office party. I invited Bob to come and join us. Jimmy would come out of his office, sit with everyone and tell stories. His business manager's son worked there too. At the time, the son was taking an acting class at U.C.L.A. He asked Mr. Stewart if he could give him any advice. Stewart said, "Learn your lines!"

I worked there for about nine months until my phone rang again. Ann Hyatt offered me a permanent production position in Disney's newly formed Home Video Division. When I told Mr. Stewart I was leaving, he wished me well and said, "Walt [Disney] was a good friend of mine." That phone call was the life-changing one they always talk about.

While working for Mr. Stewart, the Annual Santa Barbara Film Festival gave him a lifetime achievement award. Since I had made most of the arrangements for him to attend, I got us tickets. The actor Robert Mitchum was chosen to present Jimmy with the award. Mitchum said, "I owe my career to Jimmy Stewart. When I told my mother I wanted to be an actor, she said, 'If that long, tall, drink of water, Jimmy Stewart, can win an academy award, you can certainly work as an actor.'"

In his acceptance speech, Jimmy attributed his popularity to his fans and expressed gratitude for making him famous. After the event, we saw him in the lobby, and he was surprised to see me and said, "Well, gosh darn...."

In the next chapter, Bob talks about being cast in a play at the Odyssey Theatre.

BOB IN MARIE AND BRUCE

Wallace (Wally) Shawn, the actor/playwright, wrote the play *Marie and Bruce*. Wally Shawn is a character actor who played Diane Keaton's ex in Woody Allen's *Manhattan*. In *My Dinner with Andre*, Shawn received critical acclaim, a film people loved or hated.

At the beginning of Shawn's play, Marie, played by Anne Bronston, berates her husband, Bruce, played by Sam Anderson, with an almost unending tirade in which she calls Bruce every foul curse word imaginable. Bronston had a busy TV and film career before and after the play's run. Anderson already had a healthy acting career before this play. The exposure he received furthered his career. One of his memorable roles was that of an educator who made love to Sally Field in the movie *Forrest Gump,* thus ensuring the future of her son Forrest's education. And Sam Anderson, in real life, was indeed a nice guy.

The Odyssey Theatre was one of the most respected theatres in Los Angeles. They had three stages and could have three plays running simultaneously. When I read in *DramaLogue*, that there was an open audition for *Marie and Bruce,* I jumped at the opportunity. At the time, I thought I was a pretty hot method actor.

When I got to the audition, the line of actors was daunting. There were about fifteen roles up for grabs. I stuck it out and got to read for several different parts. Ron Sossi, the theatre's artistic director, directed the play. He was an award-winning director who gave up a successful TV executive career to create the Odyssey Theatre Ensemble. I didn't know at the time about Sossi's TV career; a friend later told me she had worked with him at ABC TV.

At that first audition, I must have done something right because a few days later, I got a call-back. It was an intense second audition that went late into the night. Once again, they had me read several parts with different actors each time. After that, there was a subsequent round of call-backs. To get that far in the audition process was already a big win for me.

I got the role of Antoine, an argumentative character. In the opening scene, I played opposite Mark Lowenthal, who was at least a head taller than me. We looked like a Mutt and Jeff act. Interestingly, Lowenthal had the same theatrical agent as Jack Nicholson. He would say that his agent only represented Nicholson—and him.

They built an impressive set for the play that had a movable wall. Some of us moved the wall following Marie's first act tirade, and it transposed the stage into a completely different setting.

The play opened to a sold-out house. As Ron Sossi pointed out, "One of the advantages of working at The Odyssey is our large subscriber base." That ensured the theatre had an audience on opening night because those folks had already paid for their tickets. Despite Marie's profanity at the beginning of the play, which turned some people off, it was an enormous success, and we had full houses for the entire run. We also received excellent reviews in all the local papers, which helped.

Wallace Shawn flew out from New York to see his play on the opening weekend. He was such a sweet guy. He praised and thanked each one of us for being in his play. We went out for drinks with him after the show and got to know him better. Wally was down-to-earth and sincere.

As the play got closer to the end of the run, Sossi wanted to extend it a few more weeks. One Sunday, we did a matinee followed by an evening performance. Sossi took us all out for ice cream following the matinee. We returned and had a cast meeting in which we agreed to extend the play. I was happy because I loved being in a hit production and enjoyed working with my fellow actors.

The cast was full of accomplished actors as well as newbies like me. We hung out together a lot after performances. One night, we joined some members of the *Mother Courage* cast playing next door in one of the Odyssey's other theatres. We all went to a party in a loft in an industrial part of Downtown Los Angeles. Anita joined us. It was during the punk music era. People who were dancing would jump up and bounce off the walls. It was hysterical.

During the run of *Marie and Bruce*, a funny coincidence occurred after one of our shows. Roscoe Lee Browne came backstage after the show to shake our hands and congratulate us on an impressive performance. Yes, the same Roscoe Lee Browne who years earlier came backstage to talk to the actors in *Gate 11*. Roscoe must have genuinely loved theatre.

I never worked at the Odyssey again. Years later, there was an audition with Ron Sossi for another play. (The theatre had moved from the old space to a new location a couple of miles away on Sepulveda Boulevard.) I prepared a monologue for the audition. I tried to do the monologue with an accent. It was so bad that Sossi stopped me and had me start over without the accent. It went so sour that I must have blanked it out of my mind because I don't even remember what I had chosen for a monologue. That was the last time I saw Ron Sossi. It was also an excellent example of the difficulties of being an actor with its ups and downs.

In the following chapters, Anita talks about her Disney job and the cars she owned.

ANITA'S FIRST DISNEY OFFICE

I left my job with Jimmy Stewart on a Friday and started work at Disney on Monday. This was during the reign of Michael Eisner, Jeffrey Katzenberg, and Frank Wells as studio heads. They took Disney from hard times into an industry leader. With all the new hires, growth, and an uptick in film production, office space on the Burbank lot was at a premium.

My first office on the studio lot was in a double-wide trailer with the rest of the Home Video production staff. Trailers scattered around the lot housed other Disney employees. Most of the Home Video Division was in the Fairmont Building on Riverside Drive, a short distance from the studio. Bill Mechanic headed up the new division.

The production arm of Home Video fell under the Home Video Marketing Department. The production staff created commercials and marketing materials for domestic movies released on video. We took the promotional material they used for the theatrical release of movies or animated features and adapted it for the video market. The marketing people had to sign off on the products my cohorts and I produced. Sometimes they wanted changes. That frustrated me because marketing didn't always understand the amount of time and money that went into creating those marketing tools.

Disney had a reputation as a frugal employer as far as salary goes, and they expected you to put in long hours; however, they offered an impressive benefits package. After several years of freelance work, with no benefits and sometimes not receiving regular paychecks, I was pleased with my salary and benefits. An additional perk Bob and I enjoyed was screenings and parties for new Disney movie releases.

As a new employee, I had to go to Disneyland as part of my orientation. They took me on a park tour, including the Disneyland underground. That's where all the Disney character costumes and dressing rooms were kept. I even got to go out into the park as Chip of Chip and Dale fame. I enjoyed that, especially the smiles on the children's faces and when they wrapped their arms around my legs.

The company would have an employee-only night at Disneyland for the holiday season. What a treat that was. We could enjoy the park without the crowds and lines. The park stores and some of the restaurants were open. I received a generous discount, and it was an excellent time to do holiday shopping. I bought Bob a brown aviator's leather jacket one year using my discount. He wore that jacket for years, even with holes in most of the pockets. He said, "Putting anything into those pockets meant they could disappear forever in the jacket's lining."

Of course, we could go to any Disney park for free. There were also discounts at the Disney hotels. We always enjoyed taking our young grandsons to the park. Once, we stayed in the Disneyland Hotel and took the kids to the characters' breakfast, where they could get up close to Goofy, Donald, Mickey, and many other characters. The kids loved it.

There were also some impressive holiday parties for Home Video with great food and entertainment. They always featured a great band for listening and dancing. The parties were small at first but continued to grow in size each year, reflecting the continued growth of Home Video. At a holiday party at a beach club in Santa Monica, one of my young employees, who became an entertainment lawyer, introduced Bob to Jeffrey Katzenberg. Afterward, Bob said, "I'm sure Katzenberg wouldn't know me from Adam if we met again. But it was nice to meet someone of his stature."

The Home Video organization eventually grew so large that they held their parties at the Beverly Hilton Hotel in Beverly Hills. They were in the International Ballroom—the same room where the Golden Globe Awards were held.

Since I'm talking about holidays, I should mention one in particular. That's when we got our second bird. We went to our favorite bird store to buy our cockatiel, Sushi, a bigger cage. A colorful, overly friendly, and very loud sun conure befriended Bob, and we bought it. I told Bob, "It knew a sucker when it saw one." It's difficult to tell the sex of these little birds, but the store owner told us it was a male. It was around Christmas, so we named it Natale, that's Christmas in Italian. So, instead of getting a new cage, Sushi got a new acquaintance. At first, he didn't like the newcomer but eventually became tolerant. While sitting on my shoulder, Natale laid an egg one night. We were astonished that Natale was a girl, and we started to call her Nattie Girl, or just Nattie. On our next trip to the bird store, Sushi got his new cage.

I didn't spend much time at work in my windowless, tightly cramped office. The tables, shelves, and floor contained stacks of videotapes of projects in the works or recently completed. I spent most of my time out of the office at video editing houses and working with a handful of independent producers at their offices. Bob used to laugh whenever he visited me at the office because I would be watching some video in fast forward.

I admired a window to nowhere one of my coworkers had in his office in the same trailer. He gave me the window for my office. On the wall behind my desk, I hung the old wooden window with dimensions about one foot six inches high and two feet wide. It had cracked and peeling light green paint, dried flowers, and shrubbery in front of the glass.

The job pressure, stress, and long hours became apparent immediately. Most projects were a high priority. My days were sometimes sixteen or eighteen hours long, but this was the work I had gone back to school for. I enjoyed it and tried not to complain.

After a while, our production office moved to one of the buildings on the studio lot, only to move again months later to the Fairmont Building with the rest of the divisions' employees. Management recognized my work ethic—and raises and promotions followed. The fledgling new division went through several different name changes. At first, they called it Disney Home Video, then Buena Vista Home Entertainment, and finally, Buena Vista Home Entertainment International when they expanded into the international market.

ANITA'S CARS

This seems like a good time to tell you about my cars. With all my success at Disney, I decided to buy a used 1978 Mercedes 450SL from our mechanic, Electroleon. But I didn't always drive around in such luxury.

I needed a car when I relocated to Los Angeles in the early seventies. Bob was still living in San Francisco at the time. Someone I worked with at CBS in New York had moved from the Bay Area. He sold me for one dollar his 1965 Plymouth Belvedere. It wasn't much to look at. It was black, had four doors, and was roomy. My girlfriend, Janet Bart, and I flew to San Francisco to pick up the car. A friend of Bob's from New York was visiting him. So, the four of us drove the car back to Los Angeles.

Considering its age, it ran pretty well for a while and got me back and forth to work. One evening, I was driving home from CBS Television City. We were living in Laurel Canyon at the time. The Plymouth died in the middle of the intersection of Crescent Heights Boulevard and Sunset Boulevard, one of the busy crossroads in Hollywood. I was beside myself until some guys at the gas station on the northeast corner noticed my peril and ran out to help. They pushed the car onto the gas station lot.

Whatever the problem was, they were able to get it running again. In the meantime, we went looking for a new car. I bought a brand new 1975 Datsun B210. It was small and blue. It fit four passengers but not comfortably. Of course, the insurance for the new car would be much more than I was paying on the old jalopy. I wondered how I was going to come up with the insurance money.

The following weekend we planned to take the Plymouth to the junkyard to see what we could get for it. The night before, Bob dreamt that we junked the car, took the money to Hollywood Park horse racing track, and won a lot of money. So, that's what we did that Saturday.

The junkyard gave us fifty dollars. We had a fun day at the racetrack; we won and lost some races. Towards the end of the day, we decided to play the Exacta. We bet the number five horse and the number two horse. The race went off, and at the finish, the number five horse came in second, and there was a photo finish for the winner between our number two horse and another one. We were excited. People around us were egging us on, saying, "I think you got it... I think you got it."

When the photo-finish was displayed, the number two horse won. Then, we had to wait to find out what our winnings would be. After several tense minutes, it flashed on the board. The amount was two hundred twenty-five dollars. Bob and I were jumping up and down and screaming. We got more encouragement from those around us. Then, I realized I had won the money I needed for the new car insurance. We weren't gamblers, and we never had another day at the track like that.

I mentioned earlier that the Datsun could hold four people. We took it to Mammoth, California, for a ski weekend. The normally five-hour trip took six hours probably because of the four passengers, including luggage and ski equipment. The little car strained going up into the higher altitudes. It kept dropping into a lower gear to do the climb, and we could feel and hear the engine revving. It was an experience.

After a few years with the car and sometime between working at Playboy and Jimmy Stewart, I took a job on an independent film in the Torrance area. I was craft services on the movie and had to shlep food and a big ice chest with drinks and ice.

It had rained during the night, just enough to loosen the oils secreted on the previously dry roads. As I drove around one of the bends on Laurel Canyon, the car skidded and crashed into a high curb on the other side of the road. The crash bent the left rear wheel and axle. I had to call Bob to come and help me. We transferred everything into Bob's car, they towed the Datsun away, and I drove Bob's car for the rest of the shoot. Rather than fixing the Datsun, we decided to junk it.

That's when we found a brand new 1995 Ford Thunderbird. I thought we got a good deal because it was a display model. It was a nice-looking two-door car with a blue exterior and beige seats inside. It was roomy and comfortable, with plenty of power under the hood.

My mom was visiting us and wanted to go to Las Vegas. An old friend of Bob's worked at the Golden

Nugget and got us a good deal on rooms. My mom loved playing the slots, and she was happy.

Our friend also helped us get tickets to see Willie Nelson at Caesar's Palace amphitheater. Bob and I went to the concert and had a great time. It was the first time we had seen one of Willie's shows. On the way back to downtown and the Nugget, the traffic on the Vegas strip was heavy and slow. The car started to overheat. We had to pull over and park. Bob went in the back door of one of the casinos to get water for the vehicle. He refilled the radiator, and we managed to get safely back to the Nugget before it overheated again. A service truck came to the Nugget's garage and replaced our water pump the next day. The car had one problem after another. Electroleon was our mechanic, and we usually had to bring it back several times before the trouble was repaired.

One of the consistent problems was the electric windows. We replaced the motors for those two large front windows many times. Leon showed us how small the motors were to move those windows up and down. Another time, we had to replace the car's central computer. Leon was good at finding cheap used parts and tried to keep our costs down. He always claimed we were like family.

I was fed up with the car and wanted something without the computers that came in new vehicles. Leon had a Mercedes that he said would be more reliable. He had reconditioned the 1978 Mercedes I mentioned at the start of this. It took him nine months of late nights and weekends to complete that restoration. He had fixed the car up for his wife to drive, but she didn't like it. He said she was claustrophobic and wanted a bigger car. He got her a big white Mercedes sedan that made her happy. Leon sold us the other Mercedes for seventeen-thousand dollars, and he got the owner of the car wash next door to buy the Thunderbird for his daughter.

So, I was driving this newly restored, black convertible, 1978 Mercedes 450SL. It was a 450 model, but I think Leon replaced the trunk door with one from a 500SL because that's what it said, and it also had a red stoplight on the trunk door, which a 450 didn't have. One of the benefits we found when it needed repairs was that Leon had lots of extra parts leftover from his restoration, which he would usually use.

We did fun things in that car, and it was great to drive. One day, Bob said, "I was driving down Sunset Boulevard near one of the Bel Air gates, and next to me in another Mercedes convertible was Jack Nicholson. I waved and said, 'Hi Jack!' He smiled and waved back."

We loved driving up the Coast Highway at night with the top down. On a trip to Hearst Castle, a belt broke that had something to do with emission control. The AAA mechanic who came to help said we didn't need it and got us on our way.

The car turned heads. We had it for many years until we donated it to a PBS station. The day they picked it up, it was hailing as the flatbed truck driver put it on the truck, and tears were rolling down our cheeks. We still miss that car.

In the next chapter, Bob tells you about our many skiing adventures.

SKIING OVER THE YEARS

My attraction to skiing started in the days before I left New York. I don't know why I liked skiing so much. I didn't enjoy cold weather, and many ski days can be freezing. People I worked with skied, and so did my friends. Some of them rented houses in Vermont and the Catskill Mountains for the season. Their stories about their adventures in ski country tweaked my interest. Maybe that's why I took up the sport.

Anita had skied a couple of times until she fell and had a concussion. Her mother had warned her about skiing anymore. "I'll kill you if you get hurt!" she said. Anita ignored her mom's threat and came with me on that first trip to Hunter Mountain in Upstate New York. My friend Bob Santos, a fellow student at NYU, was a skier and tried to teach me how to ski. I fell so many times on the first day that I wore the cord off my corduroy pants. On another trip to Hunter Mountain, Anita and I picked my daughter up and took her with us to Hunter. It was her first ski trip, and she enjoyed it. I was thrilled about introducing her to skiing.

Besides teaching me the basics of skiing, Bob Santos helped me purchase my first boots and skis. The salesman picked out a good-sized ski for me at the ski shop. But Bob insisted on a much longer one, claiming,

"He'll grow into it." The salesman disagreed, but I went along with Bob's recommendation. I didn't know how difficult those long skis would be and would prevent me from advancing in the sport. I struggled with them for a few years. And, skiing back east is difficult anyway because you have to deal with icy and hard-packed snow conditions.

When the ski shop called to say that my equipment was ready for pickup, Bob and I decided to skip classes that night to get my skis. We surprised Jane, his wife, when we showed up at their home. Jane made us dinner with the only thing available—veal and carrots. We laughed about veal and carrots for years after. While we waited for dinner, I tried on my boots and skis while Bob pushed me down their carpeted hallway.

When I moved to California, I learned to really ski because the conditions were much better; you skied on soft snow and not the hard-packed icy conditions back east. Living in San Francisco, Anita and sometimes our friend Janet would fly up, and we would usually head to the Tahoe area for a weekend of skiing.

I decided it was time to trade in the pontoons I was skiing on for a shorter ski. Wow! What a difference that made. My skiing improved by leaps and bounds.

When I moved to Los Angeles, our ski trips were to Mammoth in the Sierra Mountains. Anita, Janet, and I rented a ski cabin for the season. It was next to one of the ski area lodges and chairlifts. It was a cute little cabin with two bedrooms, a bathroom, kitchen, and living room, and we had a cord of firewood piled on the front porch.

That year, we would make the drive every Friday night and come back on Sunday. We even took a week's vacation. Mammoth was one of those places blessed with large volumes of snow. On the first morning of our vacation, we had our suitcases open on the bed, and we were putting clothes into the dresser. Outside it was snowing heavily. One of the ski area's snowplows was clearing the parking spaces on the street behind our cabin. Suddenly, our bedroom window was pelted with debris from the snowplow's blower. We were amazed the window didn't break. But the window did break on his return pass, resulting in three inches of snow covering the bed and floor. I had to shovel most of the snow out the broken window. We boarded up the window, moved our belongings and bedding to the living room, and slept in front of the fireplace for the next few nights.

It snowed for days. When there was finally a break in the weather, the window repairman came up to replace the broken glass. But the respite was short, and the snow started to fall again, continuing for several more days. We were getting cabin fever. One night, we couldn't take it anymore and decided to walk to a nearby bar for some drinks. The snow was thick and blinding, but we got there only to discover that the bartender was closing up. We balked, "What!" He changed his plans and stayed open for us. Trekking back to the cabin was more treacherous than our trip to the bar. We huddled close to each other, it was difficult to walk and breathe, and Janet panicked. She was hyperventilating, but we made it, and getting out of the cabin was beneficial. When the storm finally passed through, we were able to go skiing.

Then, we had the problem of Janet's car, which was buried under several feet of heavy snow. We went out with brooms and shovels to dislodge it. Janet was upset that her new car was under all that snow. With perseverance, we shoveled and swept away the heavy white stuff. Suddenly, I noticed the black vinyl top of the car was under my feet. We uncovered the trunk—most of the car was still buried in the snow. I told Anita and Janet, "I think I can go through the trunk, start the car, and back it out." I was able to fold the back seat down from the trunk and make my way to the driver's seat. Fortunately, the car started immediately. I reversed it and backed out of the snow, freeing the vehicle. We went out for dinner and drinks that evening to celebrate in town.

Not all our ski trips were like that. When I worked for Computer Sciences, they had employee ski trips that we went on. We rode in a chartered bus to Mammoth and stopped for take-out dinner along the way. The trip included a condo for the weekend and breakfast and dinner food to cook.

Sometimes, we would rent a condo with friends for a weekend. Don Kline and Penny did that with us several times. When Anita was at Disney, they had a ski club that organized trips to Mammoth. We enjoyed those, too. Some of our other ski trips took us to Aspen, where we skied that mountain, Aspen Highlands, and Snowmass. We also met our old ski buddies from back east at Park City and Aspen. It was fun skiing with my ski mentor Bob Santos again. By then, I was a pretty good skier.

We wanted to ski one winter at Vail, Colorado, or Taos, New Mexico. I went to this big warehouse sporting goods store that had a travel department. I inquired about those trips. They quoted me a price of around seven hundred dollars for either of them. The salesman said, "The best deal this year is Crested Butte, Colorado. For two hundred ninety-nine dollars, it includes roundtrip airfare, transportation to and from the local airport, a room in a bed and breakfast, ski passes for the week, and if you don't want to bring your equipment, they'll give you skis, boots, and poles." I had heard about Crested Butte, but we had never been there. I thought it was quite a deal.

Anita was suspicious and didn't trust it, but it was real. We flew out of LAX to Salt Lake City for a stopover. We didn't have to get off the plane. The final destination was Gunnison, Colorado, a thirty-five-minute drive from Crested Butte. We had a cold but wonderful week of skiing and enjoyed the town's many benefits.

We fell in love with the place, and it changed our lives. Then, one summer, we learned how beautiful the area was at that time of year, and we bought a condominium on the mountain. We would get out there whenever we could and had dreams of someday being ski bums in that lovely town.

In the next chapter, Anita talks about her move to international marketing.

ANITA GOES INTERNATIONAL

At Buena Vista Home Entertainment International, the marketing group needed a production arm. They offered me the position of Manager of Production. I was excited about this new opportunity but reluctant at first, afraid I wouldn't be able to do the job. But I couldn't turn it down. My boss was Robyn Miller, who headed up marketing for International. We had a new President, Michael O. Johnson, who came from the sales team.

I liked my new job and the people I worked with. Anticipating an increased workload, I focused on building my staff. I brought along my secretary, Nancy Dietrich, who worked for me in Domestic Marketing. I had been a secretary for many years and had high standards. Nancy filled the bill nicely for several years. But things were moving quickly in the international market, so to keep up with the steady pace, I needed a production assistant and promoted Nancy to the job. That opened up the secretarial position. None of the people I hired were as efficient as Nancy, and the job became a revolving door. I went through a slew of secretaries, male and female. I quickly got the reputation of a Murphy Brown—the TV sitcom character who went through secretaries like pantyhose.

One summer, we took a trip to Crested Butte and camped along the way. That's when we bought our condominium in Mount Crested Butte, Colorado, for forty-thousand dollars. Real estate prices had taken a beating because lots of Texas oil money and the depressed economy led to foreclosures and people dumping their properties on the mountain and in town. The condo was on the mountain across from one of the ski lifts. We had wanted to buy a place in Mammoth for years but got priced out of that market. We had equity in our Laurel Canyon home, so we borrowed from it and paid cash for the condo. When we told our accountant about it, he balked at the selling price and said, "What's wrong with it?" We explained that the economy was at fault in that tiny town.

I mention this because, before one of our vacations to Crested Butte, I was in a meeting with Michael Johnson and said, "I'm leaving this evening for a vacation."

"Where are you going?" he asked.

"To Crested Butte, Colorado."

Johnson sat up with a surprised look on his face. "I used to live there."

That surprised me. Johnson continued, "Go see my friend Allen Cox at the Nordic Inn. I worked for him when I was in college at Western State [the local college in Gunnison]. Tell him you work for me." Johnson, an avid skier, was a ski bum and student living in Crested Butte. He graduated from Western State College. During his time in Crested Butte, he worked as the night desk clerk at the Nordic Inn in Mt. Crested Butte. As a result of the introduction, we had a long friendship with Cox and his wife, Judy.

Michael Johnson and I shared a bond we had for mountains and skiing. Once a year, just before our annual sales meetings, Johnson would take his executive staff that enjoyed skiing to Vail, Colorado, for a few days of high-end dining and instructor-guided skiing. One year, we were snowed in because of an avalanche on Interstate 70, preventing us from getting to Denver to fly to our sales meeting. Johnson arranged for one of the Disney jets to whisk us out of Eagle Airport outside of Vail to the Palm Springs area for our meetings. The rest of the staff, already in Palm Springs, was impressed with our group flying in on one of the corporate jets.

It wasn't long before they promoted me to Director. With the promotion and raise came the first of Disney's stock options. These lucrative options grew in value as Disney's financial picture became more promising. Being a director meant added responsibilities, the workload increased, and my staff grew to six full-time employees plus managing several independent producers. It also meant a greater degree of stress, and it was beginning to take a toll on my health with unexplained illnesses.

Then, my department moved to the Disney Channel Building on Riverside Drive, a few blocks from the Fairmont Building and the studio lot. I moved into a luxurious corner office on the fourteenth floor. My floor-to-ceiling windows provided spectacular views of the San Fernando Valley. My secretary sat right outside my office door.

International travel was a big part of the job. I went to the U.K. often. Nancy joined me on several trips. I also oversaw projects in Spain, Switzerland, Germany, and Japan. I had a generous expense account. Bob came with me on several trips by exchanging my first-class airline ticket for two business class tickets.

Bob and I had just returned from a vacation in Italy when I found out I had to go to Spain on business. Bob tagged along. He enjoyed meeting some of the staff from the Madrid office for lunch. Dinners in Spain began at 10 p.m. or later and lasted way past midnight. We never could figure out how the Spaniards could stay out so late and get to work in the morning. Many in Spain still practiced the traditional siesta, which may have accounted for the late nights. However, I don't believe Disney condoned the siesta tradition. On one of my trips to Spain, I attended a meeting where a Spanish gentleman of some stature questioned who this woman from the states was. They still weren't accustomed to women in executive positions. On another trip to Spain, they got a car and a driver for me and drove me to the historic town of Toledo for sightseeing.

On a trip to the U.K., Nancy and I stayed in a castle on an estate where the British R.A.F. had their headquarters during World War II. I locked horns with the British director while making the latest home video commercial during that trip.

In Japan, I met with a prominent Japanese animator. Another time, a coworker and I went sightseeing and drank sacred water from a fountain that drew frowns from the Japanese people present. We didn't know what we had done until a polite, little Japanese man pointed out our indiscretion. I also rode the bullet train to Tokyo Disneyland. The park was fun. I especially remember how the signs in the park were in Japanese and English.

Bob also came with me to Hamburg, Germany. While I worked during the day, he toured the city and museums. We stayed in an old luxurious European hotel. After a long day of sightseeing, he returned to our room and took a bath in the big tub in the marble bathroom. While relaxing in the tub, he noticed a long thin cord hanging from the ceiling next to the tub. Curious, he pulled it, and someone knocked on our door several moments later. That cord summoned the maid. He apologized for the inconvenience and went back to his bath.

My next promotion was to Vice President. That brought more stock options, a significant pay raise, and a new contract. The work pace continued to increase with the success of Disney's feature films and animated movies like *Little Mermaid*, *Aladdin*, *Toy Story*, *Nightmare Before Christmas,* and *The Lion King,* to name a few. My department produced the promotional materials for these movies in the international market. I met and worked with Stan Lee of Marvel Comics fame on one project Disney was thinking about doing with Lee.

As a Vice President, I attended senior management meetings with Michael Eisner, Jeffrey Katzenberg, Frank Wells, my management, and other top Disney executives. When Frank Wells died in a helicopter crash on a backcountry ski trip in Nevada in 1994, there was a memorial service on the studio lot. Michael O. Johnson had also been on that trip but in a different helicopter than Wells. Clint Eastwood, also along, left for Carmel shortly before the crash. Eastwood, Hollywood executives, and other celebrities spoke at the memorial on the studio lot that several hundred people attended. Bob and I went to the service. The circumstances had been sad, but seeing and rubbing elbows with some of Hollywood's iconic folks was exciting.

Wells' demise left a big hole in the studio. Initially, the board of directors wanted him to head up the studio, but he didn't want the job and recommended Eisner. Michael O. Johnson would miss Wells because they were good friends, skied together, and he was a mentor to Johnson. Sometimes with a film crew, we would record Michael Eisner or Jeffrey Katzenberg for promotional messages. They were always pleasant and cooperative. I felt terrible about Well's passing, and many employees speculated about the company's future.

Over the years, we collected lots of Disney memorabilia: posters, animation cells, character statues, and clothing. Many of these hung on our walls, and other Disney items we put on shelves or stored in cabinets. We wore Disney clothing and gifted Disney memorabilia to relatives and friends. We had also amassed an extensive video collection of Disney films and movies from other studios.

In 1996, we already owned the condominium in Mt. Crested Butte for about seven years and rented it when we weren't using it. So, with our improved economic picture, we wanted to invest in a house because if we retired to the area, we couldn't live in the condo with our birds—they had a no-pet policy.

It didn't take long to find a house we liked in Mount Crested Butte, just minutes from the ski area. It was a three-bedroom with a loft, two-and-a-half-bath, and a two-car garage on a little more than a half-acre lot with spectacular views in every direction. We closed on the house the day after Halloween. The first night we slept in our sleeping bags in our new bedroom. By then, I had set my goal to retire when I was fifty. The new house would be our retirement place.

This is the last chapter I narrate. In the next chapter, Bob tells you about schmoozing.

SCHMOOZING IN HOLLYWOOD

I'll start by saying schmoozing isn't something Anita and I are good at. But as I continued working on my writing and taking acting classes, people said networking was one of the keys to getting ahead in Hollywood. "It's a who you know business," someone told me. I started to explore ways of meeting people that could help further my career.

We tried schmoozing when we had some disposable income by attending benefits for different causes. One of them was at the iconic Hollywood Roosevelt Hotel on Hollywood Boulevard. I don't remember the organization, but it was a sit-down dinner with entertainment. We won one of the door prizes and were surprised to find out how lucrative it was. It was a case of wine, several VHS MGM classic movies, and some other things. At the end of the evening, while we waited for the valet to deliver our car, we stood next to the stack of winnings that the valet helped put in our trunk.

We met a guy about our age and his attractive girlfriend at that benefit. He told us, "We crash parties like this all the time." And he wasn't bullshitting—we continued to meet them from that night on at other events.

Around the same time, I joined Women in Film. They had just started accepting men for membership. Many of Hollywood's top women executives, agents, and managers belonged. I met several of them, and it felt like I was making in-roads. At one event at a Beverly Hills restaurant, a woman acquaintance introduced me to the actress Piper Laurie, who needed no introduction. I recognized her immediately and was thinking to myself, *Wow! Piper Laurie.* She was warm, friendly, and pleasant to talk to.

I also became active in the SAG Conservatory. Besides their seminars, they offered classes on commercials and scene study. I took some classes and regularly went to events and movie screenings. Eventually, I helped with classes operating the video camera and then as a class facilitator.

There was a big conference in Hollywood about film preservation. Anita and I both attended. Many leading directors and executives were on hand as speakers and guests. Jeffrey Katzenberg from Disney spoke at the meeting about preserving films and the question of colorizing classic films.

I also joined another organization that brought industry professionals together. There were writers, directors, producers, and a lot of actors. After a while, I realized that the people I met were either has-beens or had questionable resumes, and I was paying good money with little results. At one of their networking parties, I met a producer and a woman who convinced me to join a multilevel marketing company I got involved with for a couple of years. Even though it was unrelated to the entertainment industry, I benefitted from the training classes that helped members sell products and themselves as distributors with a downline of representatives. Selling products and bringing new people in was how you expanded your business. That experience helped me gain the confidence I needed as an actor to promote myself.

The Independent Film Project was another organization I joined. It provided resources for independent filmmakers. They put on the Spirit Awards just before the Academy Awards. These were awards bestowed upon independent filmmakers. Dawn Hudson was the executive director at the time. After that, she became the CEO of the Academy of Motion Picture Arts and Sciences.

At a Women in Film event, I met an actor named Kevin E. West. We kept running into each other at other networking venues. He was a working actor who was upfront, honest, and ambitious. I liked him and his positive approach to the business. He told me about an organization he was starting to help actors succeed in Hollywood and invited me to a meeting.

AFI FILMS & ROBERT F. LYONS

At an event at the SAG Conservatory, I met and got to talk with Vincent Price. I said to him, "I am honored to be on the same page in the Players' Directory as you." (The Players' Directory is a service of the Academy of Motion Picture Arts and Sciences that lists actors and their photos for casting purposes. Yes, the same folks who produce the Oscars. There was a fee, and they listed actors in the following categories: leading man, younger leading man, and character actor with similar categories for women. I was in leading man and character actor.) Vincent Price shook my extended hand and said, "I always forget to send in my money." That surprised me because I figured he had people to do that for him.

Before being a guild member, I missed Lucille Ball's seminars at the Conservatory. I had heard they were fun and informative. After joining SAG, I could take advantage of the SAG Conservatory, and I got to meet influential people in the business.

When I became a member, their home was a campus in the Hollywood Hills that they shared with the American Film Institute. After being at the Greystone Mansion in Beverly Hills for many years, both organizations moved to Hollywood.

Since joining SAG, I was able to audition for American Film Institute (AFI) movies. AFI students got to make a film in this two-year program. Based on how the student faired the first year if they were successful, they progressed to year two. The first film I was cast in was a period piece called *Miss Lonely Heart*, about a newspaper reporter who wrote a lonely-hearts column. I was one of the other reporters in the newsroom. Michael Dinner was the director, and Eric Roberts (Julia Roberts' brother) was the Lonely-Hearts columnist. I enjoyed the work.

Later, I was cast in a first-year student film for the writer/director Raymond DeFelitta, who wrote and directed several feature films after graduation—*Bronx Cheer, Two Family House*. His father was the famous writer/producer/director Frank DeFelitta. I played a burglar who breaks into the canyon home of a down-and-out pulp fiction writer who I discover is trying to kill himself while I burglarized the place. Larry Gross, a character actor and voice coach, played the writer. For me, it was a fun part. I was so excited that it wasn't until they gave me the entire script that I realized I was the lead actor.

Another first-year student, Nancy Wyatt, cast me in her film. Wyatt worked on CBS's Sunday Morning news program. In her movie, I played a mugging victim in this two-character story. Instead of some tough guy, it was an interesting change of pace to play a victim. The film was another excellent working experience for me.

Since leaving the Strasberg Institute, I had taken only one other acting class. A woman in a play with me recommended a class she was taking. The teacher's technique was similar to what I learned when I first started acting in Tony Barr's class. You didn't preplan your choices but reacted to what you received from the other actor or actors. I was still sorting out the techniques I had learned at Strasberg and only stayed in the class a short time.

At the Conservatory, I met Robert F. Lyons, an actor/teacher. I recognized him immediately as the star of *Cease Fire,* a movie I had recently seen. I was impressed with his incredible performance. He told us about himself and the classes he taught, and he was a breath of fresh air. He was forthright and didn't mess around with a lot of bullshit. His students called him Bobby. I was drawn to him because he was a working actor, director, and writer—auditioning and working just like his students. That was a valuable advantage to us. He was also from New York and a little older than me. I felt an immediate rapport.

Lee Strasberg chose him to become a lifetime member of the Actors Studio when he was a young actor. Lyons also studied with Stella Adler, Arthur Storch, and Milton Katselas. He had been under studio contract as a young man and had a long list of TV, movie, and stage credits. Bobby incorporated the training he had—plus practical working experience.

At the time, I felt I had the techniques I needed to work. Getting the job was a challenge. If you wanted to stand out, you had to ace auditions. Bobby taught a cold reading class and a scene study class. I was interested in cold reading, which he also referred to as the "Upper Basics."

I joined his class, which was once a week. We got sides to read with another actor who sat there like most casting directors and gave you very little to work off of. Bobby taught what an actor needs to compete, get work, and do the job well. You start by using yourself, starting with your good qualities bringing the best you have, and learning how to add to that. He felt that actors needed to have techniques and know how to use them to be effective.

The class had an impressive group of actors. As in most acting classes, you also learn much from watching the other actors. Some of the working actors that Lyons worked with are Clea DuVall, Juliette Lewis, Geoffrey Lewis, Heather Locklear, Priscilla Presley, Giovanni Ribisi, Michelle Stafford, and Michael Wiseman. Clea DuVall, Michelle Stafford, and Michael Wiseman were in my class. I loved watching them work.

DuVall and Stafford left the class eventually and were working in the business. Stafford became one of the soap opera stars on *The Young and the Restless*. Michael Wisemen was a busy actor, too. Fortunately, he continued to come to class. His confidence in himself and his ability to practically memorize scene sides especially impressed me. I loved watching him work.

The class gave me free rein over my approach to finding the character's crux and the essence of a scene. I felt confident I could use the techniques I learned to make an impression and get the job.

Bobby also helped if you had an audition coming up. You could bring the sides to class, and he worked with you to achieve the best performance. He also made himself available for private sessions with him to work on audition scenes. That was invaluable. One of those sessions helped me get a part on *Matlock*, opposite

Andy Griffith. Bobby also helped me create a demo reel of my work.

In one of his classes, I experienced a revelation. After doing a dramatic scene, Bobby said, "You know you don't have to be so serious in a dramatic scene." He explained further that if you observe Gene Hackman (*The French Connection*) doing a dramatic scene, he does it with a smile. In the movie *Mississippi Burning*, Hackman questions a guy sitting in a barber chair, and he grins during the entire scene as he queries the man while shaving him with a straight-edge razor. Bobby said, "So throw a few Hackmans' in there." After that, sometimes we would critique scenes and say, "Throw a few Hackmans' in," or "it needs a few Hackmans'," which meant smiling a little. I hope I meet Gene Hackman someday to tell him about "Hackmans'."

Shortly after joining the class, Bobby asked me if I would like to join him and Michael Wiseman for pizza after class. We went to Little Tony's Restaurant in North Hollywood. Over pizza, I told them about the novel I was trying to write but didn't know how I would end it. Bobby said, "Write the end first." I thought about that and went home and wrote an ending that I liked, despite having much more of the book to write. I'm grateful to Bobby Lyons for that suggestion. However, it worked better at the beginning of my novel *Railway Avenue*. It grabbed the reader from the start. Otherwise, the story would have unfolded differently. I feel that approach made the book better. Robert F. Lyons still teaches acting, and you can find information about him on the internet.

Bobby came to a reading of a screenplay I wrote called *Big White Bonneville*. He liked it and expressed an interest in the project.

THE ACTORS' NETWORK

From my first meeting at The Actors' Network (TAN), I was convinced that this group could help me achieve my goals as an actor. I joined when it was still a small group. Everything about it was upbeat. Since its inception, The Actors' Network's mission has been "...the intelligent and proper education of the performer." Kevin E. West spoke about the importance of clearly communicating in the industry. He also encouraged being prepared and refining your skills.

This was a good fit for me. At the time, I was in Robert F. Lyons' cold reading class. I was gaining confidence from that class, and TAN furthered those efforts. We had regular meetings where people shared their successes and information about casting and other relevant things that could help the rest of us. I learned techniques to get on the studio lots and see casting people. The network offered numerous events that brought in industry people for us to meet. We were encouraged to get together with another member and make the rounds of the various casting offices to drop off our pictures and resumes. If we got lucky, they were casting something at the time that we were suitable for, and they would ask you to stay and read for a part.

I teamed up with an actress from Iceland, who was also in the network, and we would regularly make the rounds of casting offices. Once, we met the actor Forrest Whitaker. He was in an office previously occupied by a casting director. He was pleasant and took the time to talk with us.

For a while, I volunteered as the marketing manager for TAN. I used my computer skills to help promote the organization. I took advantage of an annual event at the SAG Conservatory by placing a flyer promoting TAN on car windows in the parking lot. The conference administrators used the phone number on the sheet to call Kevin. After realizing I was the culprit, Kevin apologized, saying, "one of our over-zealous members did it." I got a call from Kevin about my misdeed.

My only wish is that I would have found The Actors' Network earlier in my career. It would have saved me lots of time, money, and frustration. TAN is the most endorsed actor's business organization in the U.S.

As a network member, I found a new agent who was submitting me and getting me out for auditions. I got the lead in a play, and that's when I also worked on the *Tonight Show with Jay Leno*. Actor friends, I introduced to the network joined and saw positive results in their careers. There are so many actors in L.A. that learning to be a professional through The Actors' Network would hopefully help you stand out among the crowd.

OUR FAVORITE PLACES TO EAT/THINGS TO DO

When we moved to Hollywood in the early seventies, there wasn't the vibrant restaurant scene that evolved years later. A good example was the lack of Italian restaurants. They had Two Guys from Italy, Two Guys from Sicily, and a few other Two Guys joints. I don't remember the food quality, but the pizza was pretty good. Better Italian would come along later. We cooked a lot of Italian food at home, so we didn't look for Italian cuisine that much.

We went to places like the Old World, housed in a building that sat on a corner of a triangular-shaped piece of land. Its entrance was on Sunset Boulevard, across from the famous Tower Records. The back of it was on Holloway Drive, a road that led to Santa Monica Boulevard to the south of Sunset. The food was pretty basic, with breakfast items, burgers, and sandwiches.

Tower Records was one of the best music stores in the city when vinyl records were king. You could spend hours browsing through the different sections, but the place was a rock and roll haven. There were listening stations all over the store where you could sample albums or your favorite bands. Everyone shopped there:

musicians, actors, comedians, and Hollywood executives. I don't recall ever seeing any famous people, but we had a lot of fun times in the store.

Mexican Food

The Sundance Saloon was an unpretentious and inexpensive Mexican restaurant with sawdust on the floor and a pleasant patio in front. It was on Robertson Boulevard on the edge of Beverly Hills. The food was classic Mexican and delicious with tacos, burritos, enchiladas, etc.

El Coyote was another one of our favorite Mexican places on Beverly Boulevard, just a few blocks east of CBS Television City in Hollywood. El Coyote always had a crowd waiting for tables, and usually, you had to wait patiently while sipping their delicious margaritas in the bar. The food was always sumptuous and delicious. They served a full Mexican menu of dishes.

A European Café

Figaro Café was a great place we enjoyed going to on Melrose Avenue in West Hollywood, right next to Beverly Hills. It had a European café atmosphere. Its walls were brown like the Brown Bars in Amsterdam, with old newspapers for wallpaper. (They call them Brown Bars because they are dark with wooden interiors, nicotine-stained walls, and ceilings.) Figaro's also reminded me of the coffee houses and cafés in New York's Greenwich Village. Our friend Jurg Ebe loved Figaro's because it reminded him of places like that in his hometown of Zurich. The menu was pretty eclectic. They gave you lots of food; it was always delicious and fun to hang out.

Delicatessens

There were several Jewish delis around town. Weby's Bakery in Studio City made sumptuous sandwiches: corned beef, pastrami, brisket, plus different types of salads. There were tables along the wall opposite the bakery counter, which had beautiful-looking cakes and bread items. When you walked in the door, the aroma tantalized your nostrils. While waiting for your lunch and sitting at those tables, it was hard not to look over at the eye-pleasing baked goods in the display case. Unfortunately, Weby's has been long gone from the Studio City scene.

Art's Deli in Studio City, another of the great Los Angeles delis, opened in 1957 using family recipes and an investment of three thousand dollars. Art was a big guy who must have enjoyed the products he offered. The walls of the restaurant had pictures of sandwiches and plates of food. Like most of its competitors, Art's sandwiches probably had a half-a-pound of meat. They had breakfast items too and a bakery. There was usually some celebrity eating there. One day, at a table next to us, award-winning actor Jack Palance sat with a script in his hands, studying his lines.

Jerry's Deli opened many years after Art's and was a much bigger operation. They had several restaurants around town: Studio City, Beverly Hills, and the Marina. The Studio City restaurant competed with Art's about a mile east on Ventura Boulevard. The food quality was equal with large, sumptuous sandwiches and breakfasts. When we went there with our friend Eric Grufman and his father, his father would ask the waitperson to bring two extra pieces of rye bread with his sandwich. He would remove half the meat and fill the two pieces of bread to take home and eat later. In addition to the deli items, Jerry's also served pizza, pasta, and some other non-traditional deli dishes.

Greenblatt's was a deli serving delicious food as an excuse for selling fine wines. This Sunset Boulevard store had an extensive collection of wine, several tables, and a deli counter that turned out delicious sandwiches, sides of chopped liver, salads, and other tasty items. You could eat there, take out, and even add a bottle of wine to your order. After ninety-five years of business in West Hollywood, they closed their doors forever. My friend, and actress, Hillary Hacker, was the bookkeeper for many years.

Cantor's on Fairfax opened in 1931. It had a bakery and a deli restaurant. It was the first deli we went to when we moved to L.A. It was a big place with two storefronts on Fairfax Boulevard. They called one room the Kibbitz Room. The waitstaff was older and had some of the testy attitudes of waitpeople at many New York restaurants. The food was always plentiful and mouthwatering. It was a popular late-night gathering place, too.

Hot Dogs and Burgers
One of the great street foods in New York is hot dogs. Pink's on La Brea Avenue in Los Angeles filled the bill. This world-famous stand started as a family hot dog cart in 1939. They featured all types of frankfurters with many different toppings and many varieties of burgers. I usually ordered two dogs, one with mustard and sauerkraut and one with mustard and Pink's homemade chili sprinkled with chopped onions.

The Tail of the Pup was a unique-looking hot dog place. It looked like a wiener in a bun, turned on its side, and faced the street. You ordered through the wide window that opened outward and up. Originally located on the spot for the Beverly Center Mall, they had to move it a few blocks away to make way for the mall construction. They served delicious hot dogs. You could eat them at the tables outside or take them away.

Inside an old railroad car, Carney's was a hamburger and hot dog restaurant. The original was on Sunset Boulevard, steps from the Comedy Store. Eventually, they opened another one in Studio City next to Jerry's Deli. They may have even been there before Jerry had opened. They made their chili which they could put on hot dogs or hamburgers. Sides of sizzling fries could accompany your selection. I liked their hot dogs and burgers. I usually ordered a hot dog with mustard and sauerkraut or one with mustard, chili, and onions. Once in a while, I ordered one with mustard and neon green relish. They also made foamy, filling malts. You could eat at tables opposite the counter and in front of the windows. At the Sunset location, those windows looked out at the Sunset Strip. In Studio City, you overlooked the parking lot.

Japanese

Before we moved to Los Angeles, Anita and I had eaten Japanese food. But living in a place with a significant Japanese community made it easy to get to know sushi and other dishes a lot better. One of our favorite places was the Imperial Palace on Sunset Boulevard. It was a large restaurant with two floors. I remember eating on the second floor. The food was delicious.

It was an excellent place to see celebrities. Penny Marshall and Rob Reiner sat in the booth next to us one evening. On another occasion, the actress Jennifer Grey dined at a table across from us. I don't remember who she was with. It may have been her father, Joel Grey.

The next place I'd like to tell you about was a drug store in Japan Town in downtown L.A. Our friend Ann Hyatt introduced us to it. One side of the place was a drug store, and the other was a lunch counter. They served Japanese bowls of noodles. The sushi was fresh, delicious, and came in a bento box for under ten dollars. We loved the place because of the quality, reasonable prices, and large portions. We would go there often, usually for lunch.

Chinese

There were several places in Los Angeles Chinatown located in downtown L.A. that we liked to frequent for dim sum. We enjoyed those that came around the restaurant with rolling carts with different dim sum items. I believe one of them was A.B.C. Seafood. If you have never tried dim sum, it's a Chinese brunch. They served different kinds of wontons, shumai, chicken feet, stuffed slices of green pepper, and spareribs, to name a few.

Mon Kee was a seafood restaurant also in Chinatown. Our friend, George Stamer, introduced it to us. We spent many fun nights there with George and his wife Marlene, who was also an actress. (George always referred to her as "she who must be obeyed.") The draw for this restaurant was different types of shellfish like crab and lobsters that they stir-fried with fresh ginger and spices. If one liked hot and spicy, they had plenty of choices.

Chin Chin on Sunset Boulevard in the Sunset Plaza section of the strip was a big favorite. They had tables inside and out. We preferred inside because it was quieter, and you weren't breathing exhaust fumes. They eventually opened a second location upstairs in a strip mall on Ventura Boulevard in Studio City. The food was always good, fresh, and plentiful. The one dish that we loved was their Chinese chicken salad. They stacked it high with strips of seasoned shredded chicken, chopped romaine lettuce, red cabbage, carrots, green onions, sliced almonds, mandarin oranges, wonton strips, and toasted sesame seeds with a tasty dressing of soy sauce and rice wine vinegar. The only other Chinese chicken salad we liked as much was at Madame Wu's in Santa Monica. We ate lunches and dinners at Chin Chin and always enjoyed the food and service.

There were a lot of fine Chinese restaurants all over town. We frequented many of them.

Thai

Los Angeles had a wealth of delicious Thai Restaurants. Our favorite was Chan Dara in Hollywood. Anita and I often met there for lunch. They made the best Pad Thai we ever had. We've tried it at other restaurants in many different places—none compared to Chan Dara. They had one that included shrimp, chicken, beef, and tofu. We liked their Thai fried rice and several of their other dishes.

Lanithai in Van Nuys was a fine Thai restaurant also. We heard it was an offshoot of Chan Dara. The quality of the food was as good as Chan Dara's.

Michael, our next-door neighbor, owned the Hollywood Sunset Strip Thai restaurant named Toi. The food was excellent and reasonably priced. The atmosphere was eclectic, and the clientele were musicians, music industry people, and actors. It was always a fun place to go.

Farmer's Market

The Los Angeles Farmer's Market was on Fairfax Boulevard behind CBS Television City in Hollywood. In the old days, it was where farmers came to sell their wares. Over the years, it became a more permanent market with different food stands for purchasing meat, poultry, produce, coffees and teas, and baked goods. You could also eat there. There was a wide variety of food choices: burgers, pizza, pasta, fish, BBQ, etc. The entire market had an open roof and different places to sit and eat.

Anita and I loved one of the places that served Creole/Cajun food. I had one of my favorite celebrity encounters there. We sat and ate at a table with four chairs, and two were empty. There was a table next to us with a couple of TV actors. An actress I immediately recognized joined them. She noticed our two empty chairs, approached our table, and put her hands on one of them. Then, she hesitated, looked at us, and said, "Oh, I'm sorry! Can I have one of these?" It was the lovely, beautiful Jennifer Aniston. I smiled and said, "Sure!" And she thanked us. At the time, she was on

Friends and already famous. It was a memorable day for me.

We saw another *Friends* cast member while staying at the San Ysidro Ranch in Santa Barbara, celebrating one of our birthdays or anniversaries. We went to dinner at the resort's superb restaurant, and Matt LeBlanc (Joey, on *Friends*) was sitting with his date at the table behind us. It didn't have the same impact as seeing Jennifer Aniston. The ranch had cozy tiny cabins situated around the lush grounds. We stayed in a big bungalow with a private hot tub for one of our anniversaries.

Santa Barbara

Since I mentioned Santa Barbara, it's a good time to tell you it was one of our favorite weekend getaways. We loved making the ninety-minute drive to what some call the American Riviera with its Spanish Colonial architecture, natural beauty, ideal weather, and restaurants serving great food and wine. We had several favorite places to stay and eat.

Villa Rosa was a bed and breakfast inside a Spanish Colonial two-story house on a quiet street just about a block from the beach. The rooms were quaint with Spanish decor. They served a tasty breakfast in the morning. You could eat in the common area or outside in the courtyard next to the pool. In the early evening, wine and cheese were available in the same place where breakfast was served. Late night, they put out a nightcap of port wine and brandy. The courtyard had a small pool and a hot tub.

El Escorial was a hotel in what used to be an apartment complex. We liked it because you got a one-bedroom apartment. It also had tennis courts and a swimming pool. During one of our stays, we played doubles with an older couple in their sixties. The man stood in the middle of the court at the net and returned any balls that came his way. She ran around in the backcourt and returned anything that went past him. Before we knew it, they beat us badly. We could also bring our cockatiel, Sushi with us when we stayed there.

There were many delicious restaurants that we liked to frequent while in town.

La Super-Rica Taqueria was a Mexican spot for fish tacos, tamales, etc. It was very popular with limited seating and reasonable prices. It was one of the places we liked to go for a quick bite after riding our bikes or playing tennis.

The Ritz was a high-end restaurant for Cajun/Creole food. We loved going there for special occasions like our birthdays and anniversaries.

Brophy Bros was a seafood bar/restaurant upstairs in the Santa Barbara marina. You could sit inside at tables, at the bar, or outside on their deck. They served a wide variety of raw and cooked seafood. You could wash down the food with their delicious drinks. Their Bloody Marys were one of our favorites. I believe the restaurant had its roots on the East Coast in the Boston area.

One of our favorite things to do was dinner on the beach and watching the sunset. There was a raw bar on the Santa Barbara pier. We would buy a whole Dungeness crab, and with a bottle of wine or bubbly, we would have a picnic on the beach and enjoy the sunset.

Ribs and Seafood

RJ's in Beverly Hills was a big place with sawdust on the floor and a large, fabulous bar that served luscious drinks. They did enormous plates of barbeque ribs, chicken, steaks, oversized appetizers, salads, and sandwiches. For dessert, they had an impressively tall chocolate layer cake. Once, at our friend Ray Forman's birthday party, his wife, Betty, bought one of RJ's chocolate cakes for the occasion. It's another L.A. restaurant that no longer exists.

RJ's had a sister restaurant on the beach in Malibu called Gladstone's. It was a scenic restaurant at the end of Sunset Boulevard on the Pacific Coast Highway. You could sit outside while waiting for a table, eat seafood appetizers, and drink sumptuous cocktails. Inside, the floor had sawdust. They offered dishes from their raw bar: clams, shrimp, and oysters. The menu was extensive, with huge portions of delicious seafood. One night, we sat across the aisle from the great actor/comedian Don Rickles and his family. One of his kids spilled a glass of water on Don. Knowing Rickle's acerbic wit, we expected the worst, but Mr. Rickles calmly complained and tried to dry his pants.

Italian

I started by talking about the lack of good Italian food in L.A. That changed over the years, and many new and delicious restaurants opened. We tried and enjoyed some of them. For our special occasions, we went to Il Cielo. We loved sitting at tables in their garden on pleasant L.A. evenings. The food and service were always outstanding. It wasn't inexpensive but always worth the splurge.

Another favorite was the Mediterranean on Sunset Boulevard at the corner of Sunset Plaza. They served delicious Italian appetizers and dishes. You could sit inside the airy restaurant or outside. I preferred inside because I didn't like eating along with the car exhaust fumes on the street. That's the only knock I could give this place. The food and service were excellent, with a wide variety of Italian dishes with freshly made pasta.

California Pizza Kitchen followed Wolfgang Puck's lead with gourmet pizzas. It became a chain, and its frozen pizzas were available in supermarkets. We liked many of the pizzas. One worth mentioning was the pizza with sliced potatoes. There were several locations around the L.A. area and eventually in other cities. We've tried many of them. The quality and prices were always excellent and affordable.

TIME TO LEAVE L.A.

In March of 1998, Anita turned in her resignation at Disney, fulfilling her dream of early retirement at fifty. Management questioned her about taking a job with a competitor, but she told them, "No. I'm retiring to the mountains."

Things seemed to be going in our favor. Anita was a Vice President. She had an office to be envied, an excellent staff, a generous expense account, and all the executive perks available, and she traveled all over the world, but the stress and the long hours were taking a toll on her health. Her usual workday went from 9 a.m. to 8 or 9 p.m. I felt sorry for her, and I was looking for a permanent position at a software company in another city, thinking a move would get her out of Disney.

I had an agent I liked, and she was getting me auditions. I was still working as a freelance technical writer and training class developer in the computer industry. Although, some of that work was drying up for me. I also wrote screenplays, regularly went to my acting class, and was active in The Actors' Network. I was happy in L.A. and would have lived there indefinitely. It felt like I was getting closer to working steadily as an actor. At least that's what I thought.

However, it troubled me that Anita was unhappy. She was seeing doctors; they were taking tests but couldn't determine the cause of her poor health, probably due to stress.

At first, our small condo in Mt. Crested Butte became our refuge in both summer and winter until we bought the house. We either flew or drove there depending on how much time we had off from work. Summer vacations consisted of hiking, biking, fishing, and eating in the local restaurants. Winters, we skied. We thought Crested Butte would be a great place to retire, but we hadn't made any definite plans until Anita decided it was time to resign.

My mother suffered a stroke over the Thanksgiving weekend of 1996 and passed away several days later. Anita, my father, and I were at the hospital in Staten Island when they took her off life-support. It was the first time I had ever watched someone die. You hang on to every breath they take, thinking it could be their last. It was a life-changing moment for me.

My mom's death left the care of my semi-disabled father to us. (He had to use crutches to walk because his hips had arthritis complicated by osteomyelitis, a bone disease he had as a child.) After the New Year's holiday, we brought him to live with us in L.A. He was adjusting to life without my mother after fifty-plus years of marriage and getting used to living with us. My mother's passing was hard on him. She was his caregiver.

Just as he seemed to be turning a corner and making a new life for himself, he too had a stroke. We were going to bed. Dad was in his room. I heard a crash and rushed into the room; he was lying on the floor between his bed and my desk, breathing difficultly. I shouted to Anita, "Call 911!" She looked at me curiously until she heard my father's labored breathing. The 911 dispatcher said, "Turn him on his side."

The EMTs arrived quickly, but it seemed to take forever at the time. We could hear their siren screeching through the canyon on their way to our house. After two days at Cedars Sinai Hospital, the doctors determined he was brain dead, there was nothing they could do for him, and they took him off life-support. The young resident who disconnected the life-saving equipment looked shocked when he noticed the heart monitor was still beeping as though my dad was still alive. He grabbed Dad's chart; he looked relieved when he realized it was my father's pacemaker that was still going. One of the terrible things about a stroke is that there are no goodbyes. They say stroke victims can hear you when you talk to them. I don't know if that's true. That was a difficult time for us, and we realized how fragile life could be.

We spent the better part of 1997 cleaning out my parent's home of thirty-three years, which was not an easy task. They had a lot and never threw anything away. Fortunately, the house sold quickly.

That's when we decided to change our lives. Anita needed to leave her high-pressure job, and I was willing to support her, which meant giving up my career goals. I had to think a lot about that. Did I have regrets? Sure, I had many. Even with my growing resume, I still couldn't make the jump from a day-player to co-starring roles. I often thought that maybe I would have been more successful in New York as an actor. But I never tried to go back there to work. Finally, I rationalized that I had worked hard at it for many years, and maybe it was time to give up. We had always wanted to live in a ski area and be ski bums. My parents' passing was the catalyst that made us take the leap.

A permanent move to our house in Mt. Crested Butte became evident. After consulting our financial advisor, we found out that we could retire comfortably in our early fifties using Anita's stock options and other investments, even before Medicare and Social Security kicked in. I planned to continue to do freelance technical writing from our new home.

We waited until we sold our Laurel Canyon house before Anita resigned from Disney. What a relief it was to her. The burden had lifted from her shoulders. Disney threw a lovely party for her at one of her favorite Italian restaurants in the Valley. The following weekend, we had a party for friends and coworkers at our house.

On the day our house closed, Anita took me and our friends John Kelly and Eric Grufman for lunch at the executive dining room in the Disney rotunda. After lunch, getting home was a nightmare because of a big accident on the 101 Hollywood Freeway. It snarled traffic in the area well into the night. That evening, we had to get to Beverly Hills to sign the closing papers for the house sale. After signing the necessary documents, we still couldn't get back into our canyon because traffic was snarled all over town because of the jammed freeway, so we went for martinis and dinner at Lola's, one of our favorite restaurants, until the traffic got better. It didn't improve much by nine o'clock. We still had to take back roads to get to the house quicker. It was a fond farewell to L.A. We were glad we were leaving.

Before she left her job, Anita stressed about the move. She questioned how we would pack everything in time to get out of Los Angeles. I told her, "Don't worry. I'll take care of it." And I did. We had terrific movers who came in and packed up all our belongings. They even packed an open-topped salt and pepper shaker with salt and pepper still inside. They used two trucks because we lived on a narrow hillside street. They parked the big moving van down on Laurel Canyon, shuttled our belongings in a smaller truck, then drove it to the big van and transferred everything. Even Anita's Mercedes went into the moving van.

After the movers left, we spent that night in a local hotel. The next day, we returned to the house, packed our car with luggage, computers, personal items, and the two birds, and headed to Colorado.

We spent one night staying at the Hilton in Saint George, Utah. We chose the hotel because they allowed pets. The birds weren't happy about driving in the car for five or six hours that first day. The hotel gave us a room at the end of a hallway so that the birds squawking wouldn't bother other guests. We ordered room service, and the young man who delivered it said, "I could hear your birds all the way down the hall."

The next day's drive was even longer than the day before. The birds had enough and let us know it. We were about an hour from our final destination, and they were beside themselves. We arrived at our new home that evening. We already had some furniture there because my friend Bob Santos and I drove a truck with furniture from my parents' house in New York to Colorado when their Staten Island house sold. The next day the moving van arrived from California. We were happy to settle in.

From that first day, every morning, we sat in a different seat at the dining room table to look at the breathtaking scenery. Our new life had begun.

Anita's timing couldn't have been better. After she left Disney, there was a reorganization of Home Video. The production arm fell under the Creative Services Department, and production no longer reported directly to marketing. Then, massive layoffs followed. Her job may have been on the chopping block.

EPILOGUE

When we left Los Angeles for Crested Butte, I had some of the same feelings as when I moved out of New York. *What the heck are we doing*? This time it was different—I wasn't doing it alone. Anita was with me, and my life was happier than it was when I headed west in the 70s. Anita was glad to be free of her executive position and stress. We hoped her medical problems would go away. Fortunately, our chosen careers didn't end when we left L.A. I had reservations about giving up my acting career. Of course, I could continue to write no matter where I lived, and I could also make money doing technical writing and training development.

Our first spring in Crested Butte, Michael O. Johnson was the speaker at the Western State College Alumni Association annual awards dinner. He extended an invitation to us. In his speech, he singled out Anita and mentioned her accomplishments at Disney several times. We met people at the dinner that became friends, including the president of the college at the time, Harry Peterson. After that, we attended functions at the school and had friends who taught there.

One of the things we loved about Crested Butte, besides the great skiing and beautiful mountains, was the Crested Butte Mountain Theatre. Before moving there, we always attended and enjoyed their performances when we were in town. Getting involved with the theatre was one of our top priorities. Kathleen Mary was artistic director/manager at the time. I read in the local paper that she was starting a writers' group. That was an excellent opportunity for me to attend the first meeting and get involved with the theatre. I would eventually run the group because Kathleen had a full plate of projects to manage.

Shortly after that, we joined the theatre's board of directors. We didn't know what a challenge that would be. This was community theatre, and like most community theatres, it was a struggle to stay financially stable. At our first meeting, Anita made an impression, and the board voted her Vice President. David Owen was President. Andrew and Suzanne Hadley were fellow board members and would become good friends. Mary Tuck, a talented actress, and theatre professional was also on the board and became a close friend. The board was understaffed, so we had to build it back to full strength. We spent a lot of sleepless nights worrying about the board and the theatre's finances.

For the 2000 New Year's Eve, David Owen bought a table for board members at the Center for the Arts New Year's Eve fundraiser held in one of the hotel ballrooms on the mountain. Before the event, Aggie Jordan and her husband, Robert DeLaurenti, hosted a cocktail party at their beautiful home in Mt. Crested Butte. Their impressive three-story house had an elevator in it. I had met Aggie before that because she had written and published a book entitled, *The Marriage Plan: How to Marry Your Soulmate in One*

Year – or Less. From that party, we became good friends. Aggie influenced my writing career and inspired me. She joined my writers' group and stayed a member until she moved to California. Our friend Margot Levy introduced us to her husband at the time, Harvey Castro, at that same party. We became fast friends and spent many enjoyable days skiing, biking, hiking, and traveling together.

Eventually, I became board president. David Owen had held that position for many years. He was more than happy to let it go. Anita and I remained on the board for nine years through good times and bad. Despite the hardships, the theatre has survived more than fifty years and is the longest continuously running community theatre in Colorado.

With all these new adventures, we still missed some things about L.A. Anita and I had lived in big cities all our lives: New York, Los Angeles, and San Francisco. Crested Butte was a small town. In small towns, some things aren't available. Italian groceries were one of them. Food for our birds was another. We would drive to Denver or Colorado Springs for a big city fix and shopping.

Our birds seemed to adjust to living at nine-thousand feet, but it probably wasn't ideal for them in the long term. They sat in front of our dining/living room windows, looking out at the beautiful expanse surrounding our house. However, they didn't like the snow; the whiteness on the ground frustrated them. They were used to the somewhat greener Laurel Canyon and warm days. In Crested Butte, you could go a long time without seeing the sun, and you wouldn't see green until sometimes as late as June, and then it was a short summer.

Sushi, our cockatiel, lived to twenty-five. We had a birthday party for him. Our friends, the Sharpes, came over with their parrot to celebrate. Over the following Memorial Day weekend, his life ran out. Nattie missed him, and we lost her not too long after. We were unprepared for that. Her life expectancy was about thirty years. As a friend pointed out—that's under ideal conditions. Living at nine thousand feet was probably not the healthiest for a tropical bird. We missed them and eventually got two cockatiels from a woman who wanted to find them a home so she and her husband could travel. Their names are Rosie and Skipper.

We considered living in Crested Butte as payback time for all the success we had in our life. I volunteered at Adaptive Sports, which helped disabled people ski, usually sitting in specially constructed sleds with one or two skis on the snow. I would go along with the client and instructor, and my job was to ski behind them and block other skiers from impinging on our client's ski line. While riding a chairlift with one disabled young man, he watched people shushing down the mountain and said, "I want to be able to ski like that someday." We encouraged him and told him he would. As I mentioned earlier, my father had disabilities and trouble walking. I hoped he would be proud of what I was doing.

Anita taught Junior Achievement to the elementary school children. Sandy Fails, a local writer, interviewed her and wrote a story about her—a Disney executive who retired to Crested Butte and worked with school kids—published in *The Crested Butte Magazine*.

Through her connection with Michael O. Johnson and our new friends at the Western State College in Gunnison, Anita helped their Publicity Director, Larry Meredith, create a promotional video about the college. They used it for recruiting students. She also helped a local named Bob Hall from the Gunnison Hospital board with several projects for the hospital.

At the first writers' group meeting, Kathleen Mary said, "Find an interesting article you can write about." In the local newspaper, a longtime local wrote about the music of the '60s and '70s and how nothing was quite like it. That inspired me to write a play about a couple from Brooklyn who lived through the '70s, '80s, and '90s. I called it *Two Lives in the 70s, 80s, & 90s.* Kathleen directed, and we did the play as dinner theatre. One of the local restaurants prepared dinners, and our board members were servers. It was a huge success. I was thrilled to see my work on stage and hear laughter from the audience. The two actors in the play were Gary Candido and Genevieve Bachman. Genevieve's performance earned her a Marmot Award for best actress that year. The Marmot Awards is a popular annual event at the theatre. It's Crested Butte's equivalent of the Tony Awards but has the stature of the Oscars. Winners receive a little statue of a golden marmot with a plaque underneath for the category, e.g., Best Character Actor, Best Male Lead, etc.

My first play as an actor in Crested Butte was Steve Martin's *Picasso at the Lapin Agile.* I played an older Frenchman. In L.A., this was a play my agent couldn't even get me in for an audition. It was one of the season's big hits at the Mountain Theatre. Angie

Hornbrook was the director, and local actors were in the play.

I was also in a fun play called *The Wind in the Willows*. My role in that one was Chief Weasel. Cindy Petito, a talented actress, directed. There were a lot of young school kids in the play. After that, I watched some of those kids grow up with a love of theatre, and many perform as adults in theatre productions. When the Marmot Awards rolled around, I won two Marmots because I tied myself for best character actor in these two plays.

Shortly after that, I played a Russian comedy writer in Neil Simon's *Laughter on the 23rd Floor,* directed by one of Crested Butte's most talented and prolific actors, Tom Mallardi. The play was about the comedy writers on Sid Caesar's TV program *Your Show of Shows*. I loved hearing Tom's boisterous laughter in the audience. When he passed away unexpectedly several years later, we renamed the theatre's physical space—the Mallardi Cabaret—in his honor.

The most fun I ever had on stage was when I was in *Rocky Horror Picture Show,* directed by Shoshana Partos. I was Dr. Scott, and I maneuvered around in a wheelchair. And for the first time, I sang on stage. That was a little disconcerting because I'm not a singer. I sang the beginning of a song, and then, thank goodness, the rest of the cast joined in. My friend Mary Tuck helped me with the singing. The fun part was the audience members, who usually went nuts during the show.

Speaking of Mary Tuck, she asked me to be in *Born Yesterday* by Garson Kanin, which she directed at the theatre. I was cast as Harry Brock, an uncouth, corrupt wealthy junk dealer. There was a lovely young lady named Willow who was living in town. Mary felt Willow was perfect for the part of Billie Dawn, a showgirl and Brock's mistress. I had worked on the card scene from the play in one of Marc Marno's acting classes and was quite familiar with the play. Mary was right about Willow, who played the classic dumb blonde to perfection. Our friends Michael Baim and his son, Trevor, were also in the play. When the Marmot Awards rolled around, Michael won one for his role. Anita was Mary's assistant director. I love Mary, and she was always fun to work with.

There were many more plays that I acted in and also wrote several plays. One of the events we launched was an evening of ten-minute plays. They were an easy way for people who wanted to get involved with the theatre, either writing, acting, or directing. The theme for the first one was *Bridesmaids in Fur*. Something with fur had to appear in the play. The ten-minute play that I wrote was about an animal trainer that marries a gorilla. It was a comedy. Mary Tuck received a Marmot Award for that one as the bride's mother. These plays were very popular and an annual tradition with a different theme each year. Anita even acted in one.

During those first few years in the Butte, Anita traveled to Florida to see her aging mom. Her mom eventually passed away in her nineties. We were happy that she had come to Crested Butte years earlier. She stayed with us when we only had the condominium. While Anita was on one of her Florida visits to see her mom, I received a letter from the Colorado Council on the Arts that my screenplay *Big White Bonneville* had won the best screenplay competition.

They gave me a fellowship and awarded me three thousand dollars. With that money and a lot of our own money, we went back to L.A. to do a short film based on my screenplay. We were producers, something we both enjoyed. The script tells Frankie Russo's story. One of the biggest days of his life turns out to be one of the worst. He has an accident with his brand new 1965 Pontiac Bonneville. When he presents his girlfriend with an engagement ring, she doesn't know if she wants to marry him. Things get worse from there.

Robert F. Lyons liked the script when I had the reading at The Actors' Network before leaving L.A., and he consented to direct and help produce a short version of the film. We would shop the short around, hoping to entice someone to finance the full-length feature film. Paolo Andres from The Actors' Network also helped us cast it with some actors from the Network. We cast Michael Wiseman from Lyons' class in the role of Al, a character I originally wrote for myself, but by the time we made the movie, I was too old for the part.

We spent the early part of 2001 traveling back and forth to L.A., casting, finding locations, equipment, and editing facilities. Anita had favors owed to her from her Disney days, and her friends at Echo Entertainment generously helped us with some equipment and editing facilities. We were happy with the final product and proud of what we accomplished. It was about a thirty-thousand dollar movie that cost us half that amount. Our plan to make it into a feature film fell flat, and I gave up after finding little interest in the movie. The film made the rounds of film festivals.

We eventually sold the condo. Our new house had appreciated already, but the stock market, where we had most of our nest egg, was losing money. First from an October collapse of the market and later following 9/11. I did a couple of technical writing projects for Xerox to earn some income. But it wasn't easy. My online communication was sketchy. I'd have to send big files to a Xerox facility in Rochester; I'd lose the dial-up connection and have to start the process all over again, usually in the middle of the night.

I realized I couldn't continue doing that. I applied for and got a job in one of the two video stores in town. Bonnie Petito Chlipala was the owner of the Flying Petito Sisters Video Store. It was a fun job. Because of my Hollywood background, I could easily recommend and discuss many of the store's movies. I did that until my friend Margot Levy talked me into working with her as a concierge at the Sheraton Hotel at the ski area. I held that job for a couple of winters and summers until a hotel guest went off on me about a botched dinner reservation, and I stopped working there at the end of the summer season.

Anita remained unemployed, but I took another job, working at the local library. I stayed at that job for seventeen years. I loved the work, and it was one of my favorite jobs. Anita eventually went back to work. She worked from four in the afternoon until eleven at night on Thursday, Friday, and Saturday. She was the front desk clerk at the Nordic Inn, just down the road from where we lived. This was the same job Michael O. Johnson, her boss at Disney, had when he was a college student.

After a while, Anita tired of the job, working nights and weekends, and wanted to work in retail. She went to work in a kitchen store until it went out of business. She got a job at Alley Hats, owned by Scott Pfister, who also owned a novelty store and a toy store just up the street from the hat store. Anita enjoyed working there at first but became bored, like most jobs, after a while.

I mentioned earlier that I transitioned to writing books. Most of the members of my writing group were working on novels. That inspired me to take advantage of their expertise, and I started to work on *Railway Avenue*, my first novel, a love story that spans the 1950s, 60s, and 70s. I completed the book in 2013. I tried to find an agent or publisher. Another writer I knew in town suggested self-publishing. At first, I published it as an ebook. Its popularity grew, and I released a print version six months later. Following that one, I completed and printed *Almost A Wiseguy,* a memoir about my friend Vince Ciacci's life of crime and his struggle to overcome drug and alcohol abuse.

Then, I dove into my old screenplays and adapted *Big White Bonneville* into a novel called *Midnight Auto Supply*. Yes, the same story as our short film *My Bonneville*. My other script, *Someday You'll Be Old,* became the next to turn into a book I called *Unassisted Living*. Mildred Meyers, the main character, leads a revolt against the City of New York and a corrupt real-estate developer when they want to tear down her tenement to make way for a condominium development. This novel has a sequel, *The Hanalei House*, set on the island of Kauai, where Mildred winds up and tangles with the same real-estate developer again. I am forever grateful to the members of my writing group for their encouragement and support.

As I write this, we no longer live in Crested Butte. We sold our house in Mt. Crested Butte five years ago and moved to Santa Fe, New Mexico. Leaving the Butte was a tough decision that two aging people had to make. We lived in Crested Butte for close to twenty years. We enjoyed every minute of it. That's probably why those years went by so fast. Just like when I moved from New York and then to Crested Butte, those same doubts about the future returned. Santa Fe is where we have decided to live our final chapter. We think…

ACKNOWLEDGEMENTS

This book was started during the Covid pandemic lockdown. I had been floundering over what to write next. This one rose to the surface, and I began putting it together. But I was frustrated about how it was progressing until my friend, and fellow writer Arvin Ram called and said he was creating the *Slate River Journal*, a literary review, and wanted me to be the first author to appear in it. I felt honored and sent him an excerpt. He liked it, and with some polishing, it was published in October 2021. That was the boost I needed to complete the project. I am most grateful to Arvin for that kick in the pants.

I must thank my wife, Anita, for her help and contributions to this book. It wouldn't have come together without her.

I would also like to thank Aggie Jordan, K.K. Roeder, and Sheila Davis for their support, invaluable editing, and suggestions that have helped me polish this work. I should also thank the members of the Tano Writers Group for their input and recommendations in the early stages of writing the book.

Asya Blue, my cover designer, has again done an incredible job and created an attractive cover.

Besides being a memoir of our time in Hollywood, the book is also a homage to the people who befriended us and helped us along the way. Many of them passed on: Tony Barr, Syd Field, Michael Sevaraid, Ed Hansen, Don Kline, Hank Miller, Ray Forman, and Margaret and Buck Kartalian. Significantly, I would like to mention Lew Dauber, who we lost to cancer. Lori Zogaib, also from the *Satin Dolls* movie, had her firstborn baby boy and suffered complications that ended her life. Lastly, our fabulous singer and actress in *Satin Dolls*, Lisa Marie Gurley, was found dead, floating in her pool in Pennsylvania. There was an investigation into her death, but we never heard the results. We are thankful to all of them, and they are missed.

I always ask my friend, Harvey Castro, to read the earliest version of my books. He's a good barometer and usually offers helpful criticism. Also, I would be remiss if I didn't thank my faithful readers, whose support and admiration keep me writing.

We would love to hear your thoughts, feelings, feedback, and comments about the book. Please email us at:

books@bobpuglisi.com

To find out more about Bob Puglisi, his other books, and to read his blogs, please go to his website:

www.bobpuglisi.com

Made in the USA
Middletown, DE
05 March 2023